## Praise for *CEO COACHING*

"*CEO Coaching: How to Grow Without Limits!* is an invaluable guide for any leader aiming to achieve extraordinary growth. Kazuyoshi Hisano's deep insights, rooted in cognitive science and his unique Gold Vision methodology, offer a transformative approach to leadership. Hisano masterfully shows how to break free from limitations and unlock the full potential within oneself and one's organization. His focus on seven core powers—imagination, confidence, involvement, Feedforward, self-awareness, execution, and autonomy – provides leaders with the tools to lead authentically and inspire true change.

This book doesn't just teach you how to lead; it redefines what it means to grow without boundaries. *CEO Coaching* is a must-read for CEOs, executives, and aspiring leaders looking to elevate their vision and drive success at all levels."

– EDWARD ABRAMOWICH, CEO & Founder,
Straits Consulting Pte Ltd

---

"Mr. Hisano presents the importance of having confidence. He helps CEOs set goals and gives the ability to realize this importance clearly in the real world. He also lets us know how to become a successful CEO who can build a sound and solid organization. This book gives you a simple, easy, and structured way to solve management challenges."

– DAVID BAE, nominated by THE JAPAN TIMES as
"100 Next-Era CEOs in Asia 2010"

"This book explains how leaders can streak to a better future by leveraging their own ingenuity and changing existing mental models about how things could be."

> – DR. JOHN TOUSSAINT, MD, Chairman Catalysis and author of *On the Mend, Management on the Mend, Beyond Heroes and Beyond the Change*

---

"This book is GOLD! The more I read it the more energy I feel! This book can be used to open so many doors. Simply fantastic. It is an honor and pleasure to support you."

> – JIM GARRICK, Enterprise Excellence Manager, A.O. Smith Water Products Company

---

"Hisano creates a powerful framework for leadership growth that delivers results. By pushing beyond comfort zones to rewire your thinking, Hisano shows you how to achieve exponential improvement."

> – ERIC C. MOLL, Chief Executive Officer, Mason General Hospital

---

"In May 2020, our company came to a standstill due to the Covid-19 pandemic, and we were forced to halt all audits. During this challenging time, I reached out to Norman Bodek, who introduced me to *Gold Vision and CEO Coaching* by Kazuyoshi Hisano. Just four months later, we experienced a remarkable turnaround. We are now busier than ever and expanding our team to meet the growing demand."

> – ALBERTO MOLINAR, CEO, Global Audit

# CEO
# COACHING

## SECOND EDITION

# CEO COACHING

SECOND EDITION

## How To Grow Without Limits

**KAZUYOSHI HISANO**

NORMAN BODEK, EDITOR

PCS PRESS

Seattle, Washington

CEO Coaching



info@pcspress.com
http//www.pcspress.com



---

Publisher's Cataloging-in-Publication data

Names: Hisano, Kazuyoshi, 1974-, author. | Bodek, Norman, 1932-, editor.
Title: CEO coaching : how to grow without limits, second edition / Kazuyoshi Hisano; Norman Bodek, editor.
Description: Includes bibliographical references and index. | Seattle, WA: PCS Press, 2025.
Identifiers: LCCN: 2024950437 | ISBN: 979-8-9872585-7-6 (hardcover) | 979-8-9872585-6-9 (paperback) | 979-8-9872585-8-3 (ebook)
Subjects: LCSH Leadership. | Executives--Psychology. | Management. | Success in business. | Communication in management. | BISAC BUSINESS & ECONOMICS / Leadership | BUSINESS & ECONOMICS / Management
Classification: LCC HD57.7 .H57 2025 | DDC 658.4/2--dc23

PCS Press
PCS Inc.
1420 5TH AVE, STE 4200
SEATTLE, WA 98101-2375
1-360-605-7508

Printed in the United States of America

---

Translated by Rie Jindo and Noriko Hosoyamada.
Edited by Nihat Karaoglu and T. V. Suresh.
Cover and book design by Bobbi Benson, Wild Ginger Press.

*To my parents Kazuo and Akiko Hisano,
my wife Seiko Hisano and my son Sho Hisano.*

# CONTENTS

# FOREWORD

---

*"Everyone is born a genius"*
~ LOU TICE

A re you a genius, and do you see others that way? We were all born a genius, yet if we don't feel so, what has happened to us? Is it possible to open that potential within you? We believe it is possible, and this book will help you develop yourself to the fullest. *CEO Coaching* is for those people aspiring to be great leaders.

Kazuyoshi Hisano will show you how to drop all your limitations and rediscover the greatness within. What you can envision and dream about for your future and plant deeply into your subconscious will bring forth amazing results.

Most of us, if not all of us, allow our limitations to prevent us from obtaining outstanding success in our lives.

When I was younger, I had no confidence in myself. I struggled in school to just get by. I became an accountant because my father and brother were accountants. I went to work with them because I felt no one else would hire me. Miraculously, it all slowly changed. I was like a *tortoise*, slowly dropping off most, if not all, of my limitations. I wish I had discovered Kazuyoshi earlier. It would have been so much easier for me.

After three years as a public accountant, I discovered the computer and was able to be one of the first in the world to automate accounting. I was 20 years ahead of Bill Gates, but my lack of confidence continued to get in my way. Luckily, I started a company on my own.

In 1979, Productivity Press/Inc. slowly grew to one of the largest business publishers in America. Once again, my lack of confidence got in the way, and after 20 years, I lost the business. If I had met Kazuyoshi Hisano back in 1979 and followed his advice, my company today would have sales of over one billion. I am sure of that.

### All I needed was:

1. An aspirational goal without any limitations.
2. To strongly believe in myself.
3. To know how to gain the support of others, but also be wary of listening to other people's advice over my own intuition.

Of course, there have been, and there are many great coaches. Then what is the difference with Hisano?

1. He believes in your unlimited potential, your ability to set and attain future goals.
2. He has worked with close to 400 CEOs and many other leaders to expand their organizations.

3. He has you stretch your imagination and set very high goals.

4. He has no agenda. Whenever I consulted with others, I always had an agenda. I would tell them what I thought they should consider doing. Hisano primarily asks you questions for you to reach deeper and deeper within yourself. He helps you drop your entire defense mechanism – to recognize your fears and to rise above them.

5. Hisano currently coaches 25 CEOs and has 400 students in his online university.

6. His work is fully supported by cognitive science, knowing how the brain works to support your goals.

7. He teaches you how to use the power of your intuition and how to allow it to guide you to your success.

Everybody wants to be successful in life. We listen to advice from others, and we try many things. Yet, most of us are still not sure what is really needed to be successful. Moreover, many of us are not even sure what we are aiming to achieve in this life.

Surely, our career is important. Family is important, we need friends, and we need to be healthy. Money is important and we need hobbies to enjoy this life. But, in many cases, we are only focusing on 2 or 3 elements of our life, and the others are left behind.

Hisano will introduce you to a whole new terminology and use other familiar words differently to get your mind to act to support your new endeavor to achieve and master your new goals. Some terms used throughout this book are:

*Gold Vision* is the title of Hisano's first book, and the term was created to explain how to succeed in life. The core of Gold Vision is to shift your comfort zone[1], a place where you feel in control of your life, to a new ideal state, to a new comfort zone that allows you to achieve your future goals. This shift takes place when you set high goals.

Gold Vision means *shiny vision like gold.* Gold Vision starts with the importance of setting a high goal.

*Feedforward Thinking* is the title of Hisano's second book. After you set a high goal, you bring attention to attaining your future goal by moving things forward. Feedforward is the skill and way of perceiving things from the future and shifting the comfort zone to an ideal future. You stop living from your past and move what happens into the future to attain your goals.

**Cause Theory** is the important element that is essential to make the goals bigger and more inspiring. You set your high goal, then introspect on your purpose to identify the *causes* that enable you to expand your goals and move you to attain them.

**Comfort Zone** – we all want to live comfortably, but challenging yourself can help you perform at your peak. Stepping outside one's comfort zone is an important and almost universal factor in personal growth. How can we

---

1  A **comfort zone,** the status quo, is a psychological state and/or a physical place where you feel in control of your life. This book covers how to envision a higher goal and how to move from living the current comfort zone to a higher one.

expect to evolve in our lives and careers if we only stick to our habits and routines? Reaching new heights involves the risk of trying something we might not succeed at. Trying new things can make you more creative.

**Cognitive Science**[2] – We use cognitive science to explain how our brain works to shift the comfort zone. According to cognitive science, our brain feels real when it has a stronger sense of reality, even if the thing you imagined is not real yet.

**RAS** – *Reticular Activating System* – is "a built-in <u>screening device</u> in your nervous system, and it <u>blocks out</u> <u>or admits information</u>, depending on whether that information is <u>important</u> to you. It's a network of cells, and its job is to determine which of the thousands of sensory messages bombarding you every second are going to get through to your awareness." – *Personal Coaching for Results* by Lou Tice

**Levels of abstraction** – The degree of detail at which a system is viewed or programmed. The higher the level, the less detail. The lower the level, the more detail. The highest level of abstraction is the entire system. As we go up the levels of abstraction, conceptualization increases, and detail recedes.

**Execution** – The ability to act and achieve. It consists of the *ability to plan*, the *ability to overcome difficulties*, and the *ability to continue with steadiness*.

---

2 **Cognitive science** is the interdisciplinary, scientific study of the mind and its processes. It examines the nature, the tasks, and the functions of cognition (in a broad sense). Cognitive scientists study intelligence and behavior, with a focus on how nervous systems represent, process, and transform information.

This book takes you on a journey that can change your life and the lives of others around you for the better. I hope you enjoy the journey.

*Norman Bodek, Publisher*

# PROLOGUE:

---

## CEO coaching that changes the *one-to-10 mindset* to the *one-to-100 mindset*

"We move toward and become like what
we think about. Our present thoughts
determine our future."
~ LOU TICE

*CEO Coaching* is written for those who aspire to be great leaders, grow their organizations, and enable themselves and all their employees to be happier and more productive. This is the book to be read by top management, executives, and business unit leaders.

By reading this book, you can expect to achieve the following six objectives:

1. Imagine the ideal company and create an attractive vision.
2. Grow the company autonomously.
3. Create ample profits.
4. Achieve your own and your employees' dreams.

5. Provide happiness to your employees and society.
6. Increase your sales 100 times.

How can you make your dream come true? How can you become a happy leader? What are the fundamental principles that are common amongst growing companies? I would like to fully discuss these topics in this book.

## What is the difference between consulting and coaching?

Many companies make good use of outside brains to help them increase sales, expand their customers, and enhance their brand. As part of such efforts, they may use consultants and coaches. Let us begin with a basic question: what is the difference between a consultant and a coach? Without being conscious of the difference, management often relies on their services to talk about its problems, doesn't it?

In my opinion, consultants are those who solve problems for you. So, with their help, your problems would be solved. Every time a new problem arises, you would talk to a consultant. Thus, your costs would be perpetual.[3] On the other hand, coaches are those who teach you how to solve your problems. They teach you how to find a problem yourself and how to solve it on your own. Therefore, those who learn with the right coach are better able to set goals and solve problems on their own. This is the big difference between consultants and coaches.

---

3 I once worked with the CEO of a two-billion-dollar company who would speak with his advisor before making any new decision. – Editor

## Why does management need CEO coaching?

Many top executives, including leaders, sole proprietors, and those who want to start an independent business in the future, have sought out a personal coach. Our CEO coaching is specifically geared toward top management. The CEO coaching that we developed is a problem-solving method for top management based on cognitive science.[4]

Why does a CEO need special coaching? Because the challenges the CEO faces are not just his/her own problems, but many of the challenges are crucial and involve the entire company. Executives must use all kinds of the company's resources to solve problems. For a coach to help the leaders achieve their goals, the coach does not only need the coaching skills but also needs the management expertise and experience.

There is a decisive difference between *personal coaching* and *CEO coaching*. Generally speaking, in personal coaching, coaches advise their clients, who in turn solve the problems while taking up the advice. In CEO coaching, a coach works with both the CEO and the company's leaders to help them align to find ways to solve their problems and achieve their goals.

## It's easier to increase from one store to 100 stores than to 10 stores

*Gold Vision* (PHP Institute in Japanese; PCS Press in English) is the first book I authored and wrote about *the envisioned*

---

4  There are many books and information available on this interdisciplinary subject of cognitive science. In this book, relevant aspects of the subject will be covered later.

*future becoming a reality.* The book's title has two meanings: setting goals for the future that are shiny like *Gold* and then achieving those goals (*Goaled*, my coined term). This book explains Gold Vision, which is a future-oriented goal-setting method.

In the book, I wrote that it is easier to multiply your income by ten than double it. To double your income, you must work twice as much or double your unit prices. However, you can't just keep working harder for a long time. You must think about the effect of increasing the market prices. No matter how determined you might be, you can only expect doubling at the most through such an approach. On the other hand, when thinking about how to increase it by ten times, an entirely new way of thinking and approach is needed. Gold Vision is the method that forces you to discover new ways and actions to guide you toward a successful implementation.

Similarly, I hope to show you how to develop the mind-set of *one to 100* in order to move the company from one million in sales to 100 million. Many companies have significantly grown with this mindset. We encourage you to free yourself from the boundaries that confine you.

For example, when Seven-Eleven Japan started, their salespeople would visit liquor store owners and entice them to change their business model from a liquor shop to a store selling foods and daily necessities. Rizap, in Japan, started as a fitness gym, simply a place for exercise. They grew by providing a series of mechanisms for losing weight, by controlling diet and building muscles, and became rather quickly the best personal training gyms in all of Japan.

Kushikatsu Tanaka was a small local skewer (meat on a stick) shop that expanded its franchise to 120 shops and went public in just seven years. Looking overseas, Facebook originally started by acquiring portraits of Harvard University female students from the student dormitory and launching a comparison service on its website. Instagram was created by 26-year-old Kevin Systrom and sold to Facebook for 800 million in just two years. By changing one's mindset, the business can go from *one to 100* right away instead of *one to 10*.

## Three Theories to enable *one-to-100*

What I want to convey in this book is the three pillars of coaching to change *the one-to-10 mindset* to *the one-to-100 mindset*.

1. Goal Theory (setting high and distant goals)
2. Feedforward Theory (living from the future perspective)
3. Cause Theory (knowing why you do what you do)

Goal Theory will be covered in this book, but if you want to know more about it, you may want to read my book, *Gold Vision*: *See Your Future; Believe in Yourself; Involve and Move People* (PCS Press).

Feedforward Theory will also be covered briefly in this book. If you want to know more about it, *Feedforward*

*Thinking: Create The Future You Want* (PCS Press) is available in English.

Cause Theory is another essential theory for executives to discover and solve problems on their own. It is the third of the core topics of this book and signifies the ability to know oneself. In this book, I will explain Cause Theory in detail. It is no exaggeration to say that by learning this concept, every executive will be able to solve every problem on their own.

## Think forward, not backward

Many business executives understand the importance of having a big dream for the future but are obsessed with the past and cannot move forward. In this regard, Cause Theory requires some caution. This theory is an approach that takes you back to your roots and formative experiences. It can dig into the past too much and could impair your ability to move forward. While this theory is very important, it might pose a great risk if you start studying it carelessly.

I hope that people first thoroughly develop the habit of thinking from the future. For that reason, I decided to begin by introducing Goal Theory and Feedforward Theory in this book. Then, I want to talk about Cause Theory, which goes back to the roots of each person. By understanding Cause Theory, you can expect a revolutionary change. You will be able to establish and maintain a big goal for your future. You can expect to enhance your ability to overcome your current difficulties, which are inevitable in life. In addition, you can improve your ability to have others' involvement, which is essential for making a big leap in business. Utilizing all these theories, you can change your mindsets from *one-to-10* to *one-to-100*. The switch to make this change can be explained by cognitive science. I will discuss it in detail in Chapter 1. I will also talk about an organization's decisive execution power, which is necessary when you want to make your organization leap forward.

## A method exists for anyone to make a company with 100 million in sales!

Silicon Valley, USA, is the place where many IT companies helped the world *go around*. It has Google, Apple, Facebook, Uber, Airbnb, Intel, and Tesla, as well as Stanford University, with a reputation for producing the greatest number of globally successful entrepreneurs. It is anticipated that they will continue to lead the world's IT industry for the next 50 years. Table 1 shows the top 30 companies in the Fortune 500 in terms of sales ranking (2024). Among the top 30 companies, the only Japanese company included is Toyota Motors.

Furthermore, only three Japanese companies are ranked in the top 100 companies. Once, Japan was regarded as number one in the world of technology. Japan led the world of communications and electronics as well as the automotive industry. Japan is now a shadow of herself.

When I visit companies in Silicon Valley, they all say the same thing, "One who rules the information rules the world."

However, many Japanese executives still don't seem to understand the importance of information, and they are not putting in the necessary efforts. Japanese companies are not spending sufficient money to acquire information, and if this attitude doesn't change, Japan will be left behind in the world.

I am not saying here in this book that companies should merely strive only to increase their sales. The company leaders started and led their companies with great ambition. I don't want them to make themselves small, but to aim for bigger sales. I think the minimum sales to strive for is one million dollars in annual sales because this is the first step to being recognized in the world. Once the company has achieved 1 million, it can aspire to achieve 100 million by using our cognitive science framework. Many companies are losing out to international competition. My desire is to reach out and help business owners who are struggling to make decent sales. I hope they will learn the mindset of *one-to-100* and strive to become highly competitive in the world.

## How *the one-to-100 management* intuitively thinks and decides!

*The one-to-100 management* refers to those executive members who have learned and can run a business with *the one-to-100 mindset*. The details will be explained in this book. Briefly, suppose you have a goal for sales of 100 million dollars (100 times current), and your brain's comfort zone already exists in the world where your goals are achieved.

Then, your reticular activating system (RAS)[5] functions accordingly. RAS is a technical term for a kind of filter that only lets information reach our conscious mind that it considers necessary from the deluge of data that inundates us. In other words, RAS is the gatekeeper of intuition. It enables judgments and decisions unconsciously for you so that your comfort zone becomes a reality.

Ultimately, intuition is the key. Management and the company as a whole require continuous decision-making. This cycle of judging and deciding is repeated thousands of times a day. The better the companies, the higher the probability of successful judgments and decisions. Conversely, the company's performance will hardly improve unless the success rate of judgments and decisions increases.

So, how can we increase the success rate of judgments and decisions? The decisive factor is how much you can feel *the sense of reality* in the world of 100 times. Although you still live in the world of *one*, you must feel *the sense of reality* in the world of *100*. When you achieve this state of mind, your brain will start making judgments and decisions toward the realization of *100*.

Furthermore, if all employees feel *a sense of reality* in the comfort zone of the world of *100*, their brains will be able

---

5  RAS - The **reticular activating system** is a short, pencil-sized piece of the brain located just above where the spinal cord is attached to the brain. It acts as the gatekeeper of information between most sensory systems and the conscious mind. It filters out unnecessary information, so the important stuff gets through. In the same way, the RAS seeks information that validates your beliefs.

to exercise their intuition to maximize their full potential. This will virtually establish the *one-to-100* goal. The same goes for *one-to-10*. The only difference is that the *one-to-100* environment requires more intuition[6] than the *one-to-10*.

In the actual business scene, top management has no time to just calmly sit and think. Even if they did have the time, there is no guarantee that such thinking would lead them to the best answers. In other words, management has no other choice but to make intuitive decisions on their own. They are responsible for the consequences, of course. We will help you understand how to use your intuition more effectively.

Such an intuitive judgment can be explained briefly as follows: intuition arises to realize the world of your goal. This is what we call *the comfort zone of the goal world*.

The comfort zone of the goal world can be defined by the following four elements.

1. The goal you have set.
2. The level of your self-efficacy.[7]
3. What your *Cause*[8] is. Is the Cause lofty and strong?
4. Who do you share your comfort zone with?

---

6 Intuition means that someone uses quick understanding to interpret but without using reasoning or perception, a snap judgment.

7 "Self-efficacy is your own estimation of your ability to cause, bring about, or make happen those things that are important to you. It's your confidence in your ability to learn, make good decisions, and think effectively." This is from Lou Tice's book, *Personal Coaching for Result*.

8 Cause is a reason for an action or condition. It is something that brings about an effect or a result, a person or thing that is the occasion of an action or state – a cause for celebration.

## Figure 1: Worldwide company sales ranking top 30 (2024).

| Rank | Company | Sales (millions) | Country/Region |
|---|---|---|---|
| 1 | Walmart | 648,125 | USA |
| 2 | Amazon | 574,785 | USA |
| 3 | State Grid | 545,948 | China |
| 4 | Saudi Aramco | 494,890 | Saudi Arabia |
| 5 | Sinopec Group | 429,700 | China |
| 6 | China National Petroleum | 421,714 | China |
| 7 | Apple | 383,285 | USA |
| 8 | UnitedHealth Group | 371,622 | USA |
| 9 | Berkshire Hathaway | 364,482 | USA |
| 10 | CVS Health | 357,776 | USA |
| 11 | Volkswagen | 348,408 | Germany |
| 12 | Exxon Mobil | 344,582 | USA |
| 13 | Shell | 323,183 | United Kingdom |
| 14 | China State Construction Eng. | 320,431 | China |
| 15 | Toyota Motor | 312,018 | Japan |
| 16 | McKesson | 308,951 | USA |
| 17 | Alphabet | 307,394 | USA |
| 18 | Cencora | 262,173 | USA |
| 19 | Trafigura Group | 224,280 | Singapore |
| 20 | Costco Wholesale | 242,290 | USA |
| 21 | JPMorgan Chase | 239,425 | USA |
| 22 | Industrial & Commercial Bank of China | 222,484 | China |
| 23 | TotalEnergies | 218,945 | France |
| 24 | Glencore | 217,829 | Switzerland |
| 25 | BP | 213,032 | United Kingdom |
| 26 | Microsoft | 211,915 | USA |
| 27 | Cardinal Health | 205,012 | USA |
| 28 | Stellantis | 204,908 | Netherlands |
| 29 | Chevron | 200,949 | USA |
| 30 | China Construction Bank | 199,826 | China |

Source: Fortune 500

By improving these factors, the RAS activates your intuition to work toward achieving your goal. By deepening your understanding of the *Gold Vision Method*, your intuition will be sharpened. Those people who are successful and those executives who achieve their goals possess excellent intuition without exception. However, there are not many people pointing out this fact. In this book, I will repeatedly talk about the importance of intuition and how to train it.

# What is CEO Coaching?

## Coaching based on cognitive science

---

"If you alter the belief, you can change
the performance."
~ LOU TICE

## Overcoming obstacles to achievement

Coaching provides support to help people achieve something. The role of a coach is to bring out the best in people so they can be successful in life. Many people think of a *coach* as a person who instructs athletes in sports. Of course, baseball or soccer coaches are respectable professionals. As a professional coach, I have coached athletes, but mainly, I have worked with people in business; most of them have been CEOs in various kinds of industries. This book covers CEO Coaching in depth.

CEO Coaching is based on cognitive science. It is coaching specifically geared to management or business leaders. Cognitive science is an interdisciplinary research field that unravels the mechanism of human cognition, and it is closely related to psychology, artificial intelligence, linguistics, anthropology, neuroscience, and philosophy.

Another characteristic of *CEO Coaching* is that it includes *Gold Vision*. Having a gold vision is a way to make your future a reality. *Gold Vision* is a way of thinking that makes your dreams come true. Anyone willing to change, not just businesspeople, can get out of their current situation and achieve what they want.

*Gold Vision* is a system that is established for more effectively using the brain and the mind based on cognitive science. In applying *Gold Vision*, people are encouraged to set goals for their organization far beyond the current status and to enhance their power to establish strategies for pursuing such goals. Management leaders will be able to perform at their best and raise the performance of their organization's members. They can expect a more vitalized organization, enhancing the performance of all their human resources, resulting in increased business performance.

Many times, managers hit a "brick wall" while trying to achieve something. This is because most people are attached to or locked into their current condition, the status quo. Cognitive science can explain this tendency of ours and help us find ways to break out, and I will touch upon it later.

People everywhere seem to adhere to the status quo. If one thinks only on their own, sooner or later they will hit this limitation. One may not be aware of it, but he/she often ends up going round and round in a circle. Of course, it is possible for people to get out of the situation, but normally they cannot. A leader can take their mind outside of this vicious circle to help them achieve their goal.

## The leader is such a lonely being

Now then, what kind of method can be effective to take the mind outside of the circle? Can you find someone in business to help you? In general, it is not so easy to find someone who can support you 100% inside the organization. One can seek an outside adviser or consultant to gain a different perspective, but they often come with their own agenda. Therefore, the leader has to sort out those factors while listening to them. They need someone whose support they can trust as a "sounding board."

The other day, I had an opportunity to talk to a CEO who recently retired from a company listed on the first division of the Tokyo Stock Exchange. He said, "Before I met you, I used to have moments when I thought that everyone inside and outside of the company was an enemy. At the least, I did not feel that they were my allies."

He didn't mean that those who were around him were conspiring against him. What he meant was that he felt that they were not as reliable as he had wished for. He continued, "When I got stuck in my thoughts and could not move forward, I was very pleased to speak with you. In only 10 or 15 minutes, my questions melted away. It changed so much."

This CEO's comment shows how leaders can be amazingly lonely beings. They are in a position where they cannot show their weaknesses. Ultimately, they have to make decisions on their own.[9] They must shoulder all the responsibilities. They often have no one else to support them. This can be quite a scary place.

However, leaders cannot do everything by themselves. The organization's unique issues are generated when it challenges itself wholeheartedly toward reaching the goal. When leading a company to generate 100 million dollars in revenue, it is necessary to mobilize the whole organization. One person can't solve all the issues needed to achieve their goals. Here lies the need for the leader to have a coach.

In some cases, they need to consult with somebody else.[10] In a way, this consulting with others is a vulnerable act that shows their weaknesses. To what extent, can they show their weakness? Leaders can disclose all their weaknesses to a coach. In CEO Coaching, the golden rule is *100% for*

---

9 In the practice of management, employees when doing something new ask permission or advice from their superiors, but CEO's, with no one above them, make their decisions on their own.

10 Yes, in America many CEOs do have coaches, consultants, to work with, but very few of them, I believe can do this *leaving their agenda outside.* – Editor

*the client.* This is the commitment to being there for the client whenever something happens to them.

CEO coaching's backbone is Gold Vision, which will contribute greatly to solving the organization's unique issues. The special aspects of Gold Vision require some techniques necessary to harness and channel people's collective powers. They are the secret powers that are covered in this book, *CEO Coaching.*

## The Seven Powers necessary for a CEO to generate 100 million in revenue

There are seven powers a leader must have to achieve 100 million in revenue. Chapters 2 through 8 will cover these powers in depth. Here is a brief description of these seven powers.

**Figure 2: Seven Powers needed by the leader to grow 100 times.**

**Power to Move the Organization** (Autonomy, Chapter 8)

**Power to Execute** (Execution, Chapter 7)

**Power to Involve and Move People** (Involvement, Chapter 4)

**Power to See the Future** (Imagination, Chapter 2)

**Power to Believe in Yourself** (Confidence, Chapter 3)

**Power to Help People See the Future** (Feedforward, Chapter 5)

**Power to Know Yourself** (Cause, Chapter 6)

Source: KAZUYOSHI HISANO AND CONOWAY, INC.

The following three powers represent the **Goal Theory** discussed in detail as the Gold Vision Method in my previous book, *Gold Vision*.

1. Power to See the Future – Imagination (Chapter 2)
2. Power to Believe in Yourself – Confidence (Chapter 3)
3. Power to Involve and Move People – Involvement (Chapter 4)

The next is the **Feedforward Theory** of the Gold Vision Method, discussed in detail in *Feedforward Thinking*.

4. Power to Help People See the Future – Feedforward (Chapter 5)

This power applies to the **Cause Theory that** I advocate.

5. Power to Know Yourself – Cause (Chapter 6)

The cause can be said to be an individual's origin or deepest values. It may be better understood as something that he/she fundamentally believes in or his/her formative experiences. I am introducing the *Cause Theory* in depth for the first time in this book.

To grow the organization's strength, we need practical capability. This is the Power to execute.

6. Power to Execute – Execution (Chapter 7)

In addition, the organization needs to operate autonomously and decentralized.

7.  Power to Move the Organization – Autonomy
    (Chapter 8)

No matter how strongly the leader says, "Work harder and harder," you cannot expect the organization to function accordingly.

We foster these seven powers in *CEO Coaching*. In other words, those leaders who expand their business 100 times do have these powers.

These seven powers are individually analyzed, defined, and discussed. The basis for all these powers is cognitive science. While cognitive science is a complex system, the core of *Gold Vision* is based on one of the findings that due to the human cognitive mechanism, we are unable to recognize and maintain two things at the same time, as often demonstrated in the following examples:

Observe these two pictures:

Paul Noth, artist

Within each you can see two images[11], but not both at the same time.

---

11  This is called a Gestalt. In this book, we will see how the mind cannot live in two worlds at the same time.

Understanding this cognitive mechanism helps us use the brain as our ally in pursuing goals.

### A management leader of the leaders, who had seven powers

Konosuke Matsushita, the founder of Panasonic, is a typical example of someone who possessed the seven powers mentioned above at high levels.

- He had a grand vision and lofty goals backed by a deep philosophy known as *the water supply philosophy*.[12] (Power to See the Future – Imagination).
- He reversed the adversity of poverty, no educational background, and a weak body constitution with his belief that he could do it and made these conditions a springboard to success. (Power to Believe in Yourself – Confidence)
- He strongly believed that he would not be able to succeed without being supported by many people and made consistent efforts to be worthy of receiving support. (Power to Involve and Move People – Involvement)
- Thanks to his ability to always look into the future, he came up with ideas for new products one after another (Power to Help People See the Future – Feedforward)

---

12  The Water Supply Philosophy means "to lower the price and difficulty for consumers to obtain something by supplying large quantities of high-quality goods at low prices, like water from the tap."

- Upon having heard the news, "Electric railways would be laid in Osaka city," he intuitively felt "It would be the electric age from now on!" Sensed that he was guided by a great force beyond his will and immediately became independent. (Power to Know Yourself – Cause).

- He worked diligently without cutting corners since his apprenticeship days and was always loved by customers and other people. (Power to Execute – Execution)

- His basic stance was to delegate everything to his subordinates with 100% trust, and for the first time in Japan, he introduced the Divisional System[13] into his company, where each business operated autonomously. (Power to Move the Organization: Autonomy)

This list is only a partial description that showed Konosuke Matsushita had the seven powers explained in this book. There are many other examples. Thanks to having all the necessary powers, Konosuke Matsushita was able to create a giant company in a very short time that became one of the world's most respectable companies. Indeed, as a management leader of the leaders, he is highly regarded not only in Japan but also around the world.

---

13 Konosuke devised and instituted a system of autonomous management, dividing his company into three verticals – the first producing radios, the second handling lighting and dry batteries, and the third producing wiring devices, synthetic resins and electro thermal products. Each corporate division had its own administration, and was in charge of its own manufacturing facilities, allowing Konosuke to delegate more responsibility, and offering managers an opportunity to learn all aspects of their business – from product development through sales. https://holdings.panasonic/global/corporate/about/history/chronicle/1933.html#corp2

## By changing the habit of saying certain words, the company has grown to annual sales of 10 billion!

Have you ever heard someone say, "I have to change?" The CEO who says "I have to change" will never change. It is because they are strongly conscious about not changing. It's like the income of a person who says, "I want to make money," but their income never increases. Those who change actually change silently. In cognitive science-based coaching, this habitual utterance is called *self-talk*. It is your own mind speaking to yourself.

The thoughts you hear in your mind continuously reinforce your daily behavior. Let's take a policy announcement speech as an example. The CEO thinks about the company and says, "This is not enough." The focus will be placed on the missing parts. By being conscious and focusing on the negatives, the company and organization will deprive itself of the ability to believe in itself. This is the exact opposite of *Feedforward Thinking*. Such a situation may result in damping the force going forward. At the worst, you might end up binding your organization to the status quo.

Let's go back to the habit of saying "must change." Isn't it more than likely to be followed by the statement "But it's hard to change?" By saying it aloud, the message that "it's hard to change" is transmitted more strongly, and it reinforces your feelings as well as those of your employees, "it would be impossible to change."

In this regard, the companies that can materialize *one-to-100* are constantly changing. They have a culture of people believing "it is natural to change." As Ichiro (who was a baseball player with the Seattle Mariners) used to say in his active days, "Every moment of accomplishment is just another milestone."

How can we stop the habit of saying "I must change" and shift to realize *one-to-100*? What is required to grow business is to increase the number of customers. That's it. How do you get more customers? It is extremely difficult to generate 1 million dollars with just one product or service. If you have 3 to 5 types of products and services, you can improve your sales substantially. There would be some variations, but in principle, you can imagine your business in such a manner.

Your organizational capabilities can respond as the number of customers for each product and service increases. At the same time, the number of employees will increase. In addition, in the process of realizing *one-to-100*, you may often need to move your offices. A normal company will almost always stay in the same place for 10 years or 20 years, but in the case of *one-to-100* companies, they may move 3 or 4 times in 10 years. They are dynamic.

Those organizations positioned to naturally enjoy these changes will achieve their vision. In the process of realizing *one-to-100*, the employees will strengthen their thoughts through their own words. In terms of cognitive science, this can be described as reinforcement for your brain.

Setting a tremendous goal and heading toward it can be said to be a "grand fantasy." You may consider it a delusion.

However, this delusion is not wild; you will keep a firm grip on the reins. You can control it. Think positive. It's something you really want, and know you have the will to get it. Wouldn't you like to stop your habit of saying, "Have to change?" Wouldn't you like to seek the *one-to-100* way and get into the realm of a grand vision? No matter how grand your aspirations for the future may be, you do not inconvenience others.

## The mind aims unconsciously for the realization of the desired state

Cognitive science is the field of studies to understand the mechanism of the brain and mind. This book delves into the inability of the brain to concurrently recognize and maintain two gestalts.

Gestalt is a term used in psychology. It refers to a holistic structure that emphasizes the totality, not a loose collection of parts and elements. Humans cannot exist in two places at the same time. Everyone has a body temperature, but no one has two temperatures at the same time. Similarly, the brain cannot recognize and maintain two gestalts at the same time.

When the brain recognizes one gestalt, it tries to maintain it. This is called the *comfort zone*. The comfort zone is the place, space, and state that you are familiar with. By using this cognitive mechanism, we are trying to make our *desired state* become our comfort zone. Then, the unconscious starts working to materialize the desired state.

The brain and mind are often considered as one entity. In cognitive science, the mind encompasses both the brain itself and the mental processes it brings out. Recent suggestions propose that other parts of the body might also contribute to cognitive functions along with the brain. Nevertheless, it is commonly accepted that the mind is closely tied to the functions of the brain.

However, people 1,000 years ago had no idea where the mind was located. When they were asked where their mind was, they would point to their heart. Probably, it was a universal reaction. In fact, for many people, the more important concern is more about the mind than the brain. Understanding the mind and the brain behind it as a whole makes it much easier to accomplish something and build friendly relationships with others.

## Shifting the comfort zone for achieving success

First, to provide an overview of the comfort zone, let's look at some examples where changing comfort zones resulted in success. Here are some combinations of cases from my clients and acquaintances.

This case is about business succession. Not always, but quite often, the second-generation presidents feel they have less power than the previous generation. In many cases, their self-efficacy is low, and they tend to feel somewhat intimidated. This feeling is often reinforced by their self-talk. The biggest problem we find is that second-generation presidents are often in a situation where they cannot set their own goals.

These second-generation presidents are generally assumed, starting at birth, to succeed the founder or a dynamic leader. Their training typically starts with an outside company, and they later join their parent's company in their late 20s to mid-30s.

If, on the other hand, they join their family business when they are young, they may be assigned first-line jobs to build their experience. When they are a little older, they may be given the position of a general manager. However, even though their positions are high in the company; they often don't feel confident.

It is no easy task for these second-generation presidents. This transition to president commonly happens with the founder's retirement or death. At this time, the second-generation successors live in a firmly established comfort zone, lacking confidence and no set goals. This includes their relationship with the people around them.

Upon becoming the second-generation president, they may be motivated to implement changes. However, quick changes are difficult because they first need to transform their relationships with those around them, one by one. Without resolving their entanglements with others, true change cannot occur.

CEO Coaching helps the new presidents resolve their relationships with the people around them and helps them move toward their new comfort zones. Even while they are in this process, of course, many things can happen in their company. They may set their new directions, which may result in the company going off course. They may purge those employees who have been with the company for a long time for not being aligned with the changes.

CEO Coaching assures such second-generation presidents that this is normal and not because they are lacking capabilities. It would be the same with anybody. This assurance helps them get the burden off their shoulders.

The second-generation presidents need to move forward with those who can work with them. They need to recognize the new comfort zone being developed together with the people around them and move the comfort zone toward their desired goal. As the comfort zone moves, some of the old employees might not be able to align with it and will naturally leave the company.

A comfort zone is not fixed. The predecessor retires and the people around the second-generation president naturally change, and a new comfort zone is established.

Consider riding a bicycle, the hardest thing is gaining the initial momentum. As you continue to persevere you soon recognize it gets easier. The same applies to the business succession. Initially, it will be difficult, but you can expect to move toward a more desirable direction as you manage to move your comfort zone.

## CEO Coaching has three pillars

As mentioned earlier, CEO Coaching has the following three pillars.

1. Goal Theory
2. Feedforward Theory
3. Cause Theory

Goal Theory and Cause Theory have been briefly discussed. We now want to introduce you to a new concept we call Feedforward. Feedback[14] is a very common practice, and we continue to make use of it. While feedback focuses on the past, shortcomings and problems to be improved, feedforward focuses on looking into the future and making changes. Compared to feedback, feedforward is a more positive and productive method.

CEO Coaching takes a futuristic approach, and Feedforward Theory is for that purpose. Among the three pillars, however, Cause Theory is the most fundamental. There's a reason why it is listed as the final part. Starting with Cause Theory often fails. It has been already mentioned that the brain cannot recognize two things at the same time. We cannot be tied to the past and at the same time look into the future. As Cause Theory inevitably takes you to your past, starting with this tends to lead to failure.

If you look to the future, you won't get stuck in the past. If you have had great achievements in the past, it may not be a problem looking back on them. However, while you are looking at the past, you can lose your power and confidence to move toward the future. People need to look at the future

---

14  An example of feedback is a judge in a dance competition giving constructive criticism after a performance.

even with the challenge and hope of doing better than in the past. This is why Cause Theory is kept to the very end.

---

**Figure 3: The System of CEO Coaching**

| Name | Contents | Main Concepts | Elements of Level of Authenticity |
|---|---|---|---|
| **Goal Theory** | Ideas and methods for fully utilizing your talent and **living with abundance and happiness** ➡ Ideas and techniques for shifting the comfort zone | **Three Powers** ➡ Power to envision the future ➡ Power to trust oneself ➡ Power to involve and move people | Levels of abstraction<br><br>Degrees of distance from from the status quo |
| **Feedforward Theory** | Ideas and methods **based on the futuristic viewpoint** ➡ Techniques to encourage others to look at the future and take actions | Feedforward<br><br>Feedforward Action<br><br>Feedforward one-on-one interview<br><br>Feedforward performance evaluation interview<br><br>Feedforward meeting | Levels of futurism |
| **Cause Theory** | Ideas and methods to **know oneself and to get closer to the genius** | Relationship between "Cause" and "Goal"<br><br>Relationship between "Cause" and "Goal" and "Self-Efficacy" | Strength of the cause<br><br>Altitude of the cause |

Source: KAZUYOSHI HISANO AND CONOWAY, INC.

Cause is an important factor that defines the goal. Nevertheless, you can also delve into the Cause by expanding your goal. Therefore, you should choose Goal over Cause, when considering your main engine.

Goal Theory is built upon two fundamental pillars: *the ability to set goals* and *the ability to believe in oneself*. Additionally, the ability to involve and movie people is introduced as a third element.

## The key: the power to involve and move people

According to cognitive science, two pillars alone of the Goal Theory should work sufficiently well. However, there are cases, in which people have difficulty moving forward with these two alone. It is not an easy task to set goals and believe in yourself. These tasks include some challenging elements. In reality, many people fail to take action and stay in the status quo. This point will be covered later.

I noticed a big difference between people who do well and those who cannot move forward. I found this was based on how they related to the people around them. Why?

Gold Vision is an approach that shifts the comfort zone, which was briefly introduced earlier, by setting goals and believing in oneself. Well then, what is a comfort zone? It is a self-image and an understanding of oneself. Many factors make up who you are. The most vital, I believe, are your connections with other people. The type of people you relate to is a large part of what defines you.

Thus, I decided to combine *the ability to involve and*

*move people* with the other two, *the ability to set goals* and *the ability to believe in oneself,* to shift the comfort zone. This is to explore who you are with and who you want to be with. At first, my concept was *the two pillars + one*, but gradually I came to realize that *the ability to involve and move people* is particularly important.

Anyone, who successfully transitions to the new comfort zone, will start progressing. As you work while interacting with the people around you, the direction you are aiming for is clarified and your confidence grows. On the other hand, no matter how good your ability to set goals and believe in yourself may be, if you interact weakly with the people around you, you will remain in the state where you continue studying eagerly and become an armchair theorist. One of the features of the Gold Vision Method is that it emphasizes *the ability to involve and move people.*

## What is the difference between CEO Coaching and other coaching?

People often ask, "What is the difference between the CEO coaching method and other methods?" In short, the answer can be summarized in three ways:

1. It is based on cognitive science. Cognitive science is the culmination of what our predecessors[15] have studied over the years.

---

15  The findings confirmed by thinkers and researchers like Lou Tice, Dr. Hideto Tomabechi, and I am indebted to what I studied from Peter Drucker, Andy Grove, and others.

2. It is based on Gold Vision, a methodology explained in this book where you pick a very high goal to be successful, learn how to build your confidence, and learn how to gain support from others. Gold Vision has been created through my own experience and theorization.
3. It addresses various aspects of management.

The aspects of management include the following: First, there are cases where I was directly involved as a manager or executive. Additionally, they reflect what I learned in the process of acquiring my master's degree in business as well as the experiences accumulated jointly with clients through my CEO Coaching services. CEO Coaching consists of these three aspects, which make it unique. It is not so easily imitated, but you can do it.

CEO Coaching requires management insight as well as a lot of experience, therefore, today, there are only a few who can successfully practice this type of coaching.

For example, someone like Mr. Kenichi Ohmae, a famous management consultant and entrepreneur, would be quite an effective coach. However, it is not hard to imagine that there are not too many people who are professional coaches and who can produce quality results even though their signboard, might say "Executive Coaching."

CEO Coaching has its specific difficulties. Almost all clients are those who have considerable experience. They have already accomplished a lot in their respective field. A CEO coach must gain the clients' trust and respect and continue to provide value so that they feel good about meeting with him/her. Professional coaches need to maintain that state. Naturally, they must continue acquiring experience and studying.

## Three merits of CEO Coaching

Although there are differences between companies, I believe that top management has five common challenges:

1. Sales
2. People
3. Financing
4. Processes
5. Innovations

Among these five challenges, sales, people, and innovations are particularly significant. CEO Coaching can address these three concerns directly. This is a great advantage.

## Merit 1: Can increase sales.

Development of products and services in addition to marketing are important factors in increasing sales. In extreme terms, what you can sell is determined before you sell it. If you are thinking, "I am not sure how much it can sell, but let's sell it," it would be difficult to succeed. If the product or the service is not likely to sell, it must be processed so that it will sell.

CEO Coaching works well in the design of products and services. While setting the goal, you imagine *the state where it is selling well*. The brain will then find ways to do that.

As the levels of abstraction are raised and your vantage point becomes higher, you will be able to come up with ideas for your products and services that you have never imagined before. (The level of abstraction means how things are conceptualized and perceived. It assumes that a concept has a hierarchy of information, and the level of abstraction denotes the amount of information defining the concept.)

By raising your perspective, you will be able to come up with ideas for the products and services you have never thought of in the past. As you develop the perspective to higher levels of abstraction, your brain will be activated and get to grasp the true nature of things.

The ideal state is that the brains of the whole team, not just an individual, work that way. Then, while each member behaves autonomously, he/she will be able to see what needs to be done. It can be compared to *Criminal Squad One* in a criminal investigation. Each member of the squad may be working independently with his or her own intuition, but because of compiling the information gathered by the team, a conclusive suspect surfaces. The ideal state brings about such synergy.

## Merit 2: Can solve the problems of the organization and people.

Let's list the elements necessary for solving a problem.

- Motivation
- Organizational change
- Leadership

These are all deeply related to the brain and mind. CEO Coaching is particularly good at approaching these, for example, motivation. When motivation is high, dopamine is secreted in the brain. How you get dopamine depends on (1) Distance between the goal and the current situation and (2) Desire – what you really want. These are two of the three requirements for *the power to see the future* in setting goals. These two represent the core of goal setting.

In many cases, the reason for low motivation is that you feel obliged to do a project someone forced you to do. If it is your own project, it likely is what you *want to* do, thus, your motivation is naturally high. However, motivation will be difficult to increase in tasks such as routine sales where you feel the effort won't make much difference in good results. Such feelings often come when you haven't set your own goals.

Incentive is often used as a measure to increase motivation. It is to provide rewards for achievement. Incentives may work well in the short term, but once it is over, things will return to the previous level of motivation or fall even further down. Viewing it as a whole, it often ends up as a zero-sum game or worse sometimes becomes negative. These measures are like injecting a shot in the arm to boost energy. Employees will be in a state of "running with a constant whip" and will have a greater tendency to feel *have to*. As a result, they become exhausted. If you want to get motivated, you need to increase your dopamine secretion. That happens when you run toward the goal you set. In addition, if your goals are aligned with your life goals, you can create higher motivation.

CEO Coaching is also good for promoting organizational change. Why is organizational change prone to failure? Because one proceeds without being aware of their comfort zone. The brain is equipped with the function of "wanting to go back where it was before." If you promote changes without being aware of this force, you may make a little progress, but you will be pushed back by the power of inertia.

If you understand the function of the brain, the transition of your comfort zone will be considerably easier. If you cannot make this transition, *one-to-100* will remain merely a dream. Ideally, the comfort zone of the whole organization is constantly moving toward the goal. Among the employees, some will move ahead, while others move later. Keeping this in mind, you can take care of each individual and move the whole organization forward.

The same is true for *Leadership*. Leadership here is the generic term for all the capabilities in an organization to accomplish something. If so, then what are the elements included in Gold Vision and CEO Coaching? They are goal setting and working with confidence as a team as well as clarifying the reasons for the goals in the first place.

In managing an organization in general, you can do so much better by incorporating futuristic *Feedforward* thinking. The question now is how to value past achievements in *Feedforward*. You first look into the future and then review the past performance. Just by changing the order of your thinking process like this, you can expect a significant positive difference.

## Merit 3: Can trigger innovations.

Innovations are closely related to the level of abstraction. By raising the level of abstraction of thinking, you or your organization will be able to see what no one has ever seen before and generate truly innovative ideas. Raising your level of abstraction is seeing things from a higher viewpoint, giving you a greater perspective.

## CEO Coaching can help the organization improve performance, expand, and start up new businesses

CEO Coaching is very effective for improving business performance, scaling up businesses, and starting up new businesses. Improving business performance means being able to sell. The interesting thing about CEO Coaching is that while it contributes to performance improvement, its causal relationship is not as easily seen. Owners are often surprised by the effect of active listening employed by the coach.

Whether they are companies with dozens of employees or companies with hundreds of employees, their business performance improves just by their president speaking with a very good coach. It is because the president changes, and that spreads to employees. In response to the changes in the president's brain, the company is transformed because the organization reflects the president's brain. This will be explained further in the next section.

CEO Coaching can also help with business expansion, for example: more and more business owners want to acquire or merge companies as part of expanding their business. The ability to freely move up and down the stairs of levels of abstraction[16] is required to succeed.

When starting a new business, a lofty vision and high levels of abstraction are required. CEO Coaching will help you obtain these abilities. It is often the case that people get a new great idea, but it doesn't translate into action. You need to take advantage of futuristic *Feedforward* thinking and use *the Power to Involve and Move People* as powerful engines to accelerate implementation.

## As the leader's caliber grows, so does the organization

We hear the expression of *the president's caliber*. This term is often referencing qualities and capabilities. However, in

---

16 We will explain the concept of levels of abstraction in detail later in the book.

this book, we want to define *caliber* as *the level of perfor-mance of the brain and the mind*. When a company grows through CEO Coaching, it changes into an organization that reflects the president's mind. This is one of the findings in cognitive science—it is known that the conditions in a person's state of mind are contagious and spread to others. By sharing a sense of reality, the team members become more unified.

I am sure that you've seen a lot of dancers in concerts and musicals perform with perfect synchronization. The performers share the same image in the brain, while the movements of the limbs react and match exactly to the brain's command. When the president has a strong sense of reality in the world of the goal, employees will start feeling that reality. This is not forced; it is a natural phenomenon.

Everyone might have an experience like this: a close friend's passionate description of a movie he/she recently watched makes you want to watch it. Sometimes you may even feel you are seeing a scene from the movie in your mind.

The leader speaks to his/her employees about a big goal, which is a grand vision. As a result, the grand vision is transmitted to employees. Eventually, the employees begin to think of this grand vision as their own. Thus, they will be able to move at the same speed as the president. Of course, the president himself/herself must keep moving.

This is a big change. However, employees normally can-not outgrow the president. Ideally, the employees should be able to go beyond the president. They should be able to grow and develop beyond the president's caliber. When multiple players surpass the president, the organization will truly change. When the whole organization is looking forward to the future with excitement, then the *one-to-100* will also come to life. In contrast, in a company where the president stays indefinitely in the same position, the *one-to-100* might be hard to achieve. The synergy might be sufficient only to grow *one-to-20*.

## Identifying the essence of a leader

There are two questions that the president, who is pursuing *one-to-100*, must answer:

1. "Why do you want to do it?" and
2. "Who are you?"

It is not enough to only change the internal organization if you want to achieve a *one-to-100* transformation. It is necessary to involve and mobilize many more people such as customers and subcontractors. For that reason, there is always a time when you must directly answer these two questions.

These are quintessential questions for top management. The president's personal drives and desires alone are not enough to achieve *one-to-100*. Management needs the support of others. Realistically speaking, smaller companies have better chances to grow *one-to-100*. They do not have as many employees and the board is not too constraining so they can use their resources as they wish. That is an ideal condition. When the annual sales go up, it becomes more and more difficult. Even if you are the owner, you must gauge other executives' feelings. The relationships between your company, society, and the community will become stronger. If sales go up to 100 million, you will be flooded with perplexing matters.

There is also the issue of rewards that the management receives. If a company with annual sales of one million had grown to 3 million, should the president be compensated three times as well? This requires some contemplation. Thus, the expansion of a company is not proportionately good for the president. Many presidents are satisfied with the current level of business. Yet, if you still want to pursue *one-to-100*, of course, you need to be able to answer the questions, "Why do you want to do it?" and "Who are you?" This applies mostly to small and medium size companies.

In a large company, the situation is a little different. In general, there is not much difference among the members about the scale of goals and causes. However, some people are strongly concerned about goals and causes. They have strong unifying power in the organization for their *grand vision*.

The Nihon Keizai Shimbun column, *During My Department Manager Days*, illustrates that those who later became presidents had conducted themselves as if they were entrepreneurs while they were section managers. Their stories may be indicative of the times, but they seemed to have behaved quite differently from others. They demonstrated a strong sense of responsibility for what they passionately carried out.

## Why is Cause[17] important?

Here is one fundamental reason why *cause* is important. There are four factors necessary for mobilizing a large number of people: authority, money, legitimacy, and supporters. For example, let's assume we are to build a pyramid somewhere. Then the most powerful factor would be to use authority. If we don't have the authoritative power, we could use money. If we have neither, then legitimacy would be the key. When many people recognize you as the leader and willingly follow you to build the pyramid, that is legitimacy.

Your *cause* can adorn you with legitimacy and help you get supporters. A good example is Martin Luther King, Jr. of the United States. He was a well-known leader of the civil rights movement in the United States famous for his speech, "I have a dream." Although he was only a minister, he soon gained legitimacy and was surrounded by many supporters. He had a strong *cause* and was able to present it well. You, too, will be able to gain legitimacy and supporters, if you have a strong *cause* and communicate it well. It will work in your favor and support your efforts to achieve the *one-to-100* goal.

---

17 Cause and purpose are very similar. Cause is the reason for the purpose and also the reason for the goal. We use cause to have you think a little differently about this.

## Reveal what you really want to do

Those presidents who pursue the *one-to-100* goal need to have a valid reason why they must be the ones to do it. How can you find the answer? What you need to do is to consciously focus on the goal and look back at the present from the vantage point of the goal. By doing so, you can see yourself better. Eventually, you will start looking into your past. However, please remember not to begin with reviewing the past first. It is important that you stick to futuristic *Feedforward* thinking first. While you continue doing so, you will come to the point where you realize your formative experience. Such an experience leads you to discover your *cause*.

It's not easy to find your own *cause*. Relentless thinking does not necessarily guarantee that you will find your *cause*; it is in many people's experiences that they suddenly realize that it was this reason they have carried on as they did, and it sinks into their minds. From the perspective of brain functioning, doing what you spontaneously want to do is your strongest ally and you can overcome any difficulties to achieve it. The problem is that most people don't know exactly what they really want to do.

If they are a founder of their own business, it is usually the case that they do not need to explore anew what that is, because they are mostly doing what they want to do already. However, when it comes to the second- and third-generation presidents, it could be challenging. As soon as they inherit or take over the founder's business, they must face what they must do in front of them. They already have the employees to deal with, and they must run the business well. Nevertheless, they must find what they really want to do, within or beside the business they are in.

Let's take an example of a president I know. This person is the founder of a successfully built company with annual sales of around 80 million over 20 years. However, one day, he began thinking that his life was all about work and no hobbies. So, he started a small resort facility in a country in the southern hemisphere. It turned out that he got quite interested in it. He continued it more like his hobby and eventually developed it into a business.

Another president said, "I want to do coaching." He became an apprentice to a professional coach and set up a coaching department in his company. Although he didn't commercialize it, he incorporated coaching into his own company's education system, which still continues to this day.

There is no need to put a lid on your feeling of wanting to do something. There may be a way to shape what you really want to do, even while running your business.

## Your brain will show you the quickest path to your dream

The brain will show you the best and shortest way to achieve your dream. You might not realize it until you look back.

When you set a goal, you feel a strong sense of the presence of the goal state, and you even temporarily move your comfort zone there. Then, several hints will start showing up in front of you.

- I feel I should read this book.
- I feel I should accept this invitation.
- I feel I should rest today.

As shown above, all sentences start with *I feel*. As you follow these intuitions of yours, you are getting closer to your goal. You don't need to contemplate one by one or prioritize what to do. If you follow what you are feeling at the moment, you can proceed.

However, be cautious, because the shortest path is not necessarily the best path. It is not right to choose a path just because it is the shortest. Sometimes the path you choose may seem like a detour, but it may be the path that takes you beyond your current goal. If your brain and mind are showing you that path, it's important to take it.

A person who is called *a great success* is one who subconsciously makes such a choice. When asked, "Why did you come here today?" You may only be able to answer, "I don't know. I just felt like it." It's okay, isn't it?

"Don't think, *feel*." This line, spoken by Bruce Lee at the beginning of the movie, *Enter the Dragon*, was later quoted in the movie, *The Matrix*. This line encapsulates it all. Of course, to truly *feel*, you must have a clear image or goal of what you want to achieve. Otherwise, just feeling aimless can lead you to be swayed by your immediate desires.

## Evolving management awareness levels

When I do CEO coaching, I place importance on understanding where the client is aiming to go as well as where they are now. It's very important to understand them when interacting with the client. The order of these questions is also important. Instead of starting with "Where are you now?" and then "Where are you aiming to go?" I start with "Where are you aiming?" and then "Where are you now?" This is *Feedforward*.

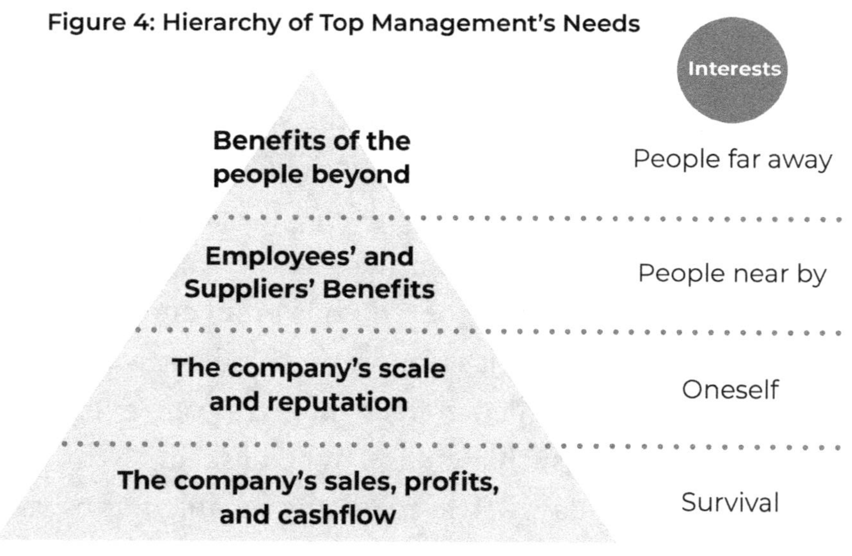

Figure 4: Hierarchy of Top Management's Needs



Source: KAZUYOSHI HISANO AND CONOWAY, INC.

In general, people start with the question "Where am I? However, this approach tends to deflect their driving force. Your progress will be faster when you confirm *where you want to go* first and then check *your current location*. This is my understanding and experience.

What you need to do is dependent on what you pursue. When you are clear about where you are heading, the gap between the company's growth stage and management's state of mind closes. What needs to be done depends upon this gap. Therefore, what I say and the nature of my advice to the client changes, based on the gap.

The following are the four stages of management's awareness level:

1. Pursuing the organization's sales, profits, and cash flow.
2. Expanding the business and branding.
3. Considering the well-being of all individuals concerned. (The stage where adequate rewards are thought for employees, staff, and business partners.)
4. Thinking of society's future benefits. (The stage where what needs to be done becomes clear.)

Panasonic and Softbank are examples of companies that grew along these stages. In particular, Konosuke Matsushita was a person with his eyes on Stage 4 from the very beginning, while he did what was required at each stage. The same can be said about Otobank, a venture company, which is run by an acquaintance of mine.

### This coaching is for team leaders, too

Regardless of your position within the company, it's important to adopt a mindset akin to top management. This will enable you to achieve overwhelming results. While CEO coaching is primarily for top management, it can also benefit team leaders.

Fostering future leaders is a crucial management responsibility. It is important to strengthen the current team leaders and develop candidates to become next-generation executives. This process is essential for companies to realize one-to-100. Thus, it is natural for many top managers to think that team leaders also should be trained in CEO Coaching.

What is happening in the mind of the executive who has successfully acquired management's perspective and been exposed to CEO Coaching? Not surprisingly, they can work autonomously and in a decentralized manner, just like business owners. Autonomous decentralization can be rephrased as self-reliant independence. Today, team leaders are required to do just that, and this trend will intensify in the future. There are several reasons.

Technological advancements have increased what you can do alone. A business owner's true perspective would be expecting these candidates to work on their own as much as they can.

Even in the manufacturing industry, the sight of working together is a thing of the past. The proportion of manual work has been steadily decreasing, and it is not uncommon for a single operator to run a large section of a factory alone. These changes are one of the factors that are accelerating autonomous decentralization like that of top management.

Availability of information is another big factor. The ground is emerging for autonomously collecting information and thinking about it on your own. In this regard, I believe, young people should be given more authority. They would be able to show their abilities and work more joyfully.

The education level of your people as a whole is rising. Anyone in the young generation can use computers and gather information on the Internet as a matter of course. In this era, pupils study programming in elementary school, in addition to traditional subjects such as language and arithmetic. The level of intellect is indeed higher than before. If you utilize capabilities well, you should be able to achieve better results.

When I worked for a company, I felt most of my dozens of subordinates were capable of doing more, but they were getting by half-heartedly. Human resources in general have potential. If you cater to their natural strengths, they will grow even more.

Recently, a division director at a major Japanese financial institution received CEO Coaching, and the institution's performance has risen rapidly since. He significantly grew as a leader due to his attitude of welcoming the coaching and considering himself as top management two or three levels higher than he was.

## The golden proportion of leadership

Gold Vision has a leadership model, with its foundation in cognitive science. It considers the keys of existing leadership theories and covers the requirements needed to create the future. In this book, the importance of futuristic thinking has been emphasized many times. On that premise, the next issue is how to shift your comfort zone. For this, the leadership model of Gold Vision comes into play.

---

**Figure 5: Gold Vision Leadership Model**

| | |
|---|---|
| Power to see the future | Indicate "Direction" |
| | Identify the "Scotoma" |
| Power to believe in yourself | "Energize" the team |
| | Elevate "Collective Efficacy" |
| Power to involve and move others | Be the "Role Model" |
| | Get "Involved" and "Grow the team" |

**Feedforward**

**Cause**

Mindset of respecting people, thoughtfulness, and considerateness.
Dedication to work and determination to achieve the results.

**Get results with model team**

---

Source: KAZUYOSHI HISANO AND CONOWAY, INC.

The existing leadership theories have some points that need to be examined, do they promote thinking from the past or looking toward the future? Here, many of the existing leadership theories in the world aim at "optimization based on the past" and, at best, "optimization based on the current situation." This is symbolized by the fact that the concept of "best practice" has been greatly valued over the past few decades. It is based on the study of past successes of other companies and then applying them to your business. The vectors in the best practice model are completely looking back at the past. If it works, you may be able to get some results for a while. However, is your business success sustainable?

Why has such a method been so popular? This is because the environment surrounding company management was relatively stable. So, we could improve our company's practices for a few years and even pretend that we were innovative. However, now it is hard for us to see what is going to happen even two years ahead. With the change in the environment so intense, how valuable would it be to learn about other companies' successes three years ago and apply them to your company?

There is a limit to the leadership theories that place importance on the past. I had the opportunity to see an article in an economic magazine, with the headline read "Unprecedented Period of Change." The first appearance of such a term was in the 1950s. Even in the middle of high economic growth, the economy had its share of ups and downs. It is better not to use 20th-century leadership theory today as is. My position is to ask the question, "Isn't it more interesting to create a future that no one has seen yet?" There's a lot to learn from history and it's interesting, but it should be kept as a topic to study or as a hobby. It is important to know that there is little that can be achieved by applying past cases to current management.

## The leader's state of mind spreads and promotes ideas widely

I already touched upon the point that the leader's state of mind is infectious and spreads as *a shared sense of reality*. Let me elaborate on this. This propagation happens at the subconscious level. Have you ever felt bad, when a frustrated person is near you and felt pleasant when you interacted with cheerful people? This *sense of reality* may be shared as shown in these examples, but there are also cases like those that follow:

I have a client who is the head of the sales department of a company. He appears to be confident but may not be. He is an athlete in his 40s. He is quite an achiever. The fact that he was selected for CEO Coaching shows that his company has high expectations for him. At my first encounter, I noticed his facial expression hardly changed. His eyes were a bit glassy. "Do people say you are scary?" I asked a leading question. "Eh?" He seemed to be surprised. I showed him a photograph of a famous writer known for his fierce look and continued, "But not this extreme." As he saw the picture of reference, he got it and commented, "This man's eyes look glassy."

What he said was that he internally felt angry at many things but tried not to show his feelings at work. He continued, "Not many people come and talk to me." I replied, "Perhaps, they are afraid of you."

He commented that he sometimes unintentionally scolded his subordinates rather harshly. This further made them fear him. He noticed that he rarely praised anybody, although he is a kind person. It was a pity that his good nature did not come across to others. I gave him the task of making his image change, so as not to be so scary.

From the perspective of cognitive science, when a boss is scary, his/her subordinate becomes timid, and the level of abstraction is lowered. When the prefrontal cortex of the brain is active, you can expect to generate creative ideas. On the other hand, in situations where people work with the fear of being scolded, the amygdala, also called "the reptilian brain," is activated. In this situation, you will be far away from creativity and your thinking is limited.

He complained that his subordinates did not positively take part in discussions. The true cause was that this leader was scary.

The state of the leader's mind is transmitted in various ways which doesn't always go in the positive direction. It is important to be aware of the negative situations.

In the following chapters, let's delve into the specific elements of the CEO Coaching framework that were discussed in this chapter.

**CHAPTER 2**

# The Power to See the Future: Imagination

---

"If you don't control your self-talk,
your self-talk controls you."
~ LOU TICE

**The Three Powers of Goal Theory**

The goal theory is supported by three powers:

**1. The power to see the future.**

---

The power to see the future is the ability to set a goal and feel the sense of reality in that goal. In this book, goals can be rephrased as objectives, dreams, visions, etc. There are three requirements to be met for good goal setting.

### a. Set it far away from the status quo.[18]

In measuring the sufficiency of this requirement, I use the term distance from the status quo. The higher the distance, the better the goal will be.

### b. Desire it as it comes from your heart.

"What I sincerely desire" can also be called "want to." The opposite concept is "have to." Whether it is something "I want to" or "I have to" is very different and wanting to is an important requirement.

### c. Set it in every aspect of life.

When we set goals in Gold Vision, we use these words: *the axis of greatness*, *the axis of want-to*, and *the axis of many*. (Please refer to *Gold Vision*.) We can address *the axis of many* by drawing a *Balance Wheel*[19]. We'll talk more about the balance wheel later. Balance wheels exist not only in individuals but also in companies. In the case of management, a balance wheel as an individual may be a little different from that for the management or the company.

---

18  The **status quo** is the current state of things. If you are rich and admired, then you're probably not interested in disrupting the **status quo**. Status quo is Latin for "existing state." When we talk about the **status quo**, however, we often mean it in a slightly negative way. as if you are stuck.

19  Balance wheel is where you will set future goals in all of the important areas of your life: career, family, finance, etc.

## 2. The power to believe in yourself.

---

It's called *efficacy* or *self-efficacy* in psychology. *Efficacy* is believing in yourself; believing in your ability to accomplish your goals.

When your efficacy is high, it becomes easier to achieve your goals. If it's low, the goals might be unattainable.

## 3. The power to involve and move people.

---

When you have set your goals high and believe deeply in your ability to achieve them, then you need to engage others. How you move in the desired direction to achieve your goals is important. You need *the power to build personal connections* or *the power to involve other people* because *a comfort zone* is mainly made up of people. The foundation of this power is in cognitive science.

## With a Balance Wheel, expand the possibility of your life to infinity

Let's dig a little deeper into the *Balance Wheel*. No matter how great a person you are, you should build a balance wheel to elucidate all of your important wishes.

In my CEO coaching sessions, I often ask the CEOs, as a first step, to write their balance wheel. I also recommend that you update the balance wheel each week in the first month and then at least once a month thereafter. I recommend these frequent updates to the balance wheel because your goals will change as you learn more about the method. Among my clients, those who have steadily updated their balance wheels are getting closer to their goals. It seems that the progress slows down when updates lag.

The balance wheel represents your *future self*. It must be something *outside of your status quo,* and you *want to.* Since you will be thinking about multiple goals in writing the balance wheel, the three requirements for goal setting will naturally be met. The balance wheel is an excellent exercise that can cover all three requirements.

However, after you reach a certain stage, you can update the balance wheel only when necessary. It's not something you "have to continually update the rest of your life." In fact, I don't even write it anymore unless there are some new things I want to learn.

## Let's get specific on how to create a Balance Wheel[20]

First, I ask people to draw a circle on a notebook, divide it into eight segments, and fill in the important items in their lives. At this time, I get them to write as many as they can. One example is shown in Figure 6. This is only an example. It's important to write what comes to your mind.

---

20  Go to "Balance Wheel Chart" in the Internet and look at the images of many different charts.

**Figure 6: Example of the Balance Wheel**

- Travel: Taking two or three long vacations every year and enjoying relaxed time in the favorite country or city.
- Touring castles: Visit castles every year where I have not been before with sufficient research.
- Golf: Playing golf twice a month with the average score 78. I'm taking lessons twice a month.
- To find new hobbies, I am actively trying to do anything.

- The entire company is united to move forward to achieving our ambitious goals.
- In the year 20XX, the company went public and became a listed company at the New York Stock Exchange.
- I am always looking for new businesses, and I am developing and launching at least one product every year in the area that no one had ever done before.
- I am succeeding my management skills and knowledge to the next

- Earning annual income of XXX dollars from the work that I truly enjoy myself.
- Have formed assets of XXX dollars in 10 years.
- Have established a philosophy of money.

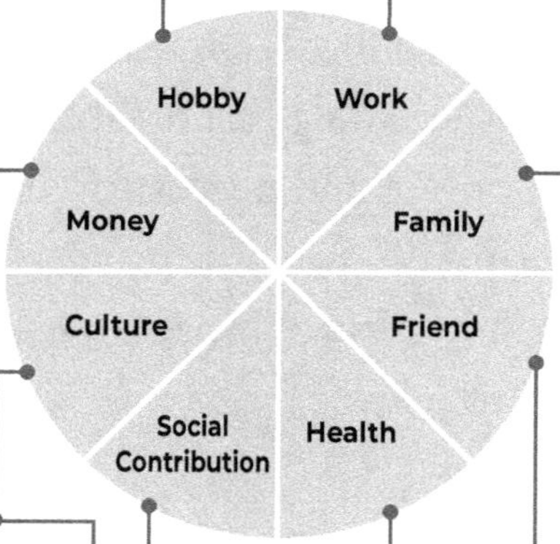


- Just being with my family makes me feel happy.
- Each member of my family is working hard to realize their dreams and they are enjoying their life.
- Family member respects each other with love.

- Studying the basics of physics in classes or through reading books.
- Deeply studying the history of Eastern Europe from books.
- Started learning philosophy.

- I am exercising several times a week.
- I am proactively eating foods that are good for health.
- I am sleeping well.
- I frequently quietly face myself to fulfill my mind.

- Providing value to society through my work.
- Making donation of XXX dollars every month to +++.
- Regularly participating in community service activities that involve physical work.

- I am spending relaxing time with my good friends several times an year.
- I have many friends in many countries.

At this stage, some people cannot fill all 8 items, and stop after about 5 items, which is not uncommon. But you don't have to worry.

Moreover, you can set these items as you feel right for you. For example, in the item "family," some people may want to create separate categories for their family whom they live with and for their parents or siblings who live independently from them, while others want to keep them together. If you have many hobbies, you might want to focus only on your hobbies. Some people think that "occupation" includes "money." However, it is recommendable to keep "money" as a separate item from "occupation," as it has both aspects of income and expenses as well as an aspect of asset formation,

Some people, as they write, end up with "mostly just about the company (*work*)." When you say "associates," you may be referring to "subordinates" or "colleagues." It is okay to focus only on "work," however, it is advisable to be aware that your Balance Wheel is skewed only one aspect of your life.

Once the eight items are filled in, I ask people to write their goals on the outside of each item. The tip here is to set goals, as far from the status quo as possible, and write them as if you've already achieved them. The brain is deceived by writing "I did" instead of "I want to." If you can't think of goals outside the status quo, write "something I'd like to happen." Some items, like *health*, make it more difficult to set goals outside the status quo. In this case, you don't have to stick to the rule.

You can't make something perfect from the beginning. Over time, you will want to rewrite it. You just need paper and a pen to write the balance wheel. However, the benefit of writing one is enormous. Incidentally, sometimes I have the opportunity to do coaching for married couples. When the husband and wife write his/her balance wheel, some of them are shocked at the huge difference between their balance wheels. I highly recommend you do this.

## How to get out of the current state of mind

When setting goals, *outside the status quo* will be the keywords. I've already mentioned this point, but let me repeat that you should be as far away from the status quo as possible. Otherwise, you will inevitably try to get through with a mindset and an approach that is closer to the status quo. The brain tries to cope while still using the thought pattern of the current comfort zone. This is not going to bring about a revolution.

Here's a simple way to enhance your distance from the status quo.

First, engage with people outside of the status quo as much as possible. This is important. Comfort zones are made up of people. They are closely tied to relationships with people who are connected to you. It's very difficult to change your comfort zone on your own. If you engage with people outside of the status quo, you can force yourself to experience it.

Another important thing to do is to "try it out when you feel like doing so" and "take action." If you cannot do it, it may be because you are caught up in the status quo. And here's what you need to accept as a premise: "I don't know everything."

For example, I know a certain amount about coaching, but of course, I don't know everything about the universe. Even if I maintain the status quo, I will sooner or later be left behind. When you think about it, you realize that you have no choice but to go outside of the status quo to explore your possibilities. As a business owner, you must keep moving forward.

## To shift your comfort zone, you don't have to "work hard"

You need no power to shift to a new comfort zone. Zero power. In the "Star Wars" movie, there is a scene where a small ship is drawn into a big ship. It's just like that. That is, you just need to create a state of gravity on the goal side. Then, all that's left to do is to be drawn into there.

However, it must be something that you like to do, so you would be naturally doing it to the fullest extent. Others may think that you are making a lot of effort. You are though just enjoying what you are doing. You may also say "Sometimes it can be physically hard, but I don't mind because this is something that I'd love to do." It is not like "Look, I am working so desperately hard." Perhaps you might have had such an experience once or twice, or even more often. Usually, you achieve better results in such circumstances.

The farther the goal is outside the status quo, the easier it will be to get closer to it. A goal of "105% year on year" is close to the status quo, and that is a tough one to achieve. If the goal is "180% year on year," then, "you will have no choice but to just do it." That means you will have to explore a completely different way to achieve it.

## The key premise is to find the *want-to-goal* that you sincerely desire

To be motivated, your brain needs to be in a state where dopamine is being secreted. For that, you need to make the goal a *want-to-goal*. Put the other way around, if you look inside the brain of someone who is acting based on *want-to*, you will find dopamine is secreted there. There is also a risk. A large amount of dopamine is also secreted in the brains of those who are addicted to gambling with a want-to mindset. It just depends on how you use it. The key is what kind of goals you set.

On the other hand, you need to be careful that a *want-to* mindset could sound like idealism. If you look at your real life, many things need to be done as *have-to* tasks. Even for the business that you started, you can't manage everything by yourself. There are a lot of troublesome and cumbersome things to do. It is important to be mindful of such *have-to* tasks by yourself. You must be aware that "I'm doing *have-to* tasks right now," but you also need to accept that it's part of a bigger *want-to* goal.

One example I often cite is "taking out the trash in the morning." I don't think many people are enjoying this and doing it as *want-to* work. For many people, taking out the trash is just a *have-to* task. So, what if you stop taking out the trash? You can't do that. This is because the garbage will pile up and it will be a big problem.

There are *want-to* goals such as "I want to keep the house clean" and "I want to feel clean," and then there is the *have-to* task of taking out the garbage, as part of the *want-to-goals*. If we change our perspective or raise our levels of abstraction[21], taking out the trash would be a part of the *want-to-goal*. The same is true for the work that you are not keen to do. It will all be *want-to* if you expand your perspective.

If raising the levels of abstraction makes it part of the *want-to*, then you should do it. I also recommend that you draw a diagram showing what kind of *want-to-goals* subsume the *have-to-goals*. On the other hand, no matter how much you try to raise the levels of abstraction, if it always remains as a *have-to*, and if you think it's a waste of time, you should stop it.

If you want to bring out the *want-to* of your employees or subordinates, the CEO needs to act in a *want-to* manner. Those around you are looking at you quite closely. If the CEO is running the business with a *have-to* attitude, it will be recognized immediately. There is no way to create a *want-to* in the entire organization if the leader has a *have-to* attitude.

At night, before going to bed, look back on the day, and feel strongly, "I was able to work on everything based on a *want-to* mindset all day." This is the ideal.

---

21 Levels of abstraction refers to having the ability to see things from a higher level where things have a different meaning.

What should you do if your workplace has a *have-to* culture? Review your work-life balance and increase your want-to mindset in areas outside of work. This is one way of thinking, but your working hours will continue to be difficult. In most cases, there should be some *want-to* in your work. It won't be zero. Why not try to increase this percentage? It's a good idea to increase the levels of abstraction and make it a *want-to-work*. Alternatively, you can actively suggest what you want to do. The important thing is the ideas and actions that lead to results. The more *want-to-work* you have the more likely you are to achieve positive results.

Here is a secret to finding *want-to* outside of the status quo. Try one or two things a month that you haven't done before. Experiencing a different comfort zone will change the way you see things.

I'll tell you one way to get through the *have-to* tasks. "Hold your breath and just do it." If it must be done anyway, let's just get it done quickly. That should be fine, right?

## The human mind instinctively seeks to maintain the status quo

The mind is always trying to slack off and take it easy.[22] It instinctively tries to maintain the status quo. In terms of sustainability of life, keeping the status quo is a reasonable decision. Seeking change will involve risk.

It may be an extreme statement, but the fact that a living creature is alive today means that what it has done until

22  You might like to read **Thinking, Fast and Slow** by Daniel Kahneman Nobel Prize winner in Economic Sciences. – Editor

yesterday was right. No wonder that we instinctively want to maintain the current state as it is.

In the case of humans, there is another fact to consider. From our childhood on the importance of maintaining the status quo is imprinted in our brain through every opportunity.

When it comes to taking the entrance exam for high school or university, you are given an idea about your chances for entrance at a certain university by your guides and recommended to pick an institution according to where you have a chance for entering, based on your current score. It seems like the career guidance you receive at school is all about revising your goals downward.

It's not just about exams. The mindset of *this level should be good enough* can be seen in many situations. Most people have grown up with *coaching with downward revision*. It might have been fine during the period of high economic growth. However, we are now in a time of uncertainty and are supposed to be living satisfying both the *want-to* mindset and *self-reliance*. It is irrational to just keep the status quo. Nevertheless, many schools seem to be continuing the status-quo-based education.

We all feel fear when we try to change. It is scary to change. The instinct of self-protection gives rise to fear of change. It's not easy to get over this fear. It won't be possible to overcome it with just a fighting spirit. Find a way to get over it. That is the Goal Theory.

It's important to note, however, that even if you think "I want to change," it does not mean that all the items listed in the balance wheel need to be fundamentally changed. Some of them are just fine as they are. Of course, even if it is fine now, there's always a possibility that it won't be so sooner or later.

The aim of this book is not to tell you that you must change. The reason is that it's your choice to *change* or *not*, and besides, the human brain becomes amygdala-dominated[23] when threatened. I'm trying to be careful that what I say with good intentions doesn't backfire. In the end, everything is a choice. If you are seriously thinking, "I like the current situation as it is," then you should be happy with that. However, you still need to make sure that you are indeed as happy as you think you are.

## The importance of re-setting goals

There is one thing more important than setting a goal. That is re-setting a goal. Why? The answer is quite simple. Because the more times you reset the goal, the higher your aim will be. Setting the first goal is a one-time affair. After that, you will repeatedly reset the goal. As a result, the goal will not be achieved even in a lifetime. Of course, the initial goal is achieved, but at that point, the goal you are aiming for is farther ahead on the line.

What is the right time to reset a goal? *When you see the steps that you need to take to achieve your goal* – that is the right time. This time comes not long after the goal is set. For

---

23  The **amygdala** is responsible for the perception of emotions such as anger, fear, and sadness, as well as the controlling of aggression. The **amygdala** helps to store memories of events and emotions so that an individual may be able to recognize similar events in the future.

example, it is said that high-end brands, such as those that represent the European apparel industry, are already thinking about their new store layout when they are selling best. It's too late to start thinking about what to do next after sales start to fall. It is in the prime of your life that you need to be prepared for the future. This is not limited to the apparel industry. The same is true for the timing to reset goals.

There is one more important thing to remember when you reset a goal. The updated new goal doesn't necessarily have to be an extension of the old goal. It is fine if the direction changes. Let's take an example of a sales goal. Once you achieved 20 million dollars, do you have to aim for 50 million dollars next? This is not necessarily the case. On the organization's balance wheel, the sales can remain 20 million dollars, and you can aim for a different goal.

In the phase where you are in pursuit of scale or sales, your focus tends only to be on expansion. But that's not what goal resetting is all about. Remember that expansion is not the only thing you need to pursue.

The timing of goal resetting does not necessarily come at regular intervals. When you set a goal that is far out of your status quo and when you have sub-goals for the goal as an intermediate point, you could check those sub-goals on a regular basis.

Example:
- **Goal:** Build a company that is truly contributing to the local community. The annual sales of the company

are 100 million dollars, and the number of employees is 400. (Don't care about the timing…)

- **Subgoal 1:** Achieve 50 million in five years. At that moment the employees are 250. We have 3 major product groups.
- **Subgoal 2:** Achieve 30 million in 3 years. At that moment the employees are 150. We have 2 major product groups.

You should check these sub-goals on a regular basis. It is because you may find a different way of doing things in the process of working toward the original goal.

## The more real it feels, the faster you will achieve the goal

Let me talk a little more about transitioning the comfort zones. We know that the brain chooses *the highly realistic world*. Also, the brain cannot maintain *two gestalts* at the same time. Let's put these two properties at the core and apply them. To realize a goal, you need to make that goal feel as realistic as possible. As a result, you can accelerate the speed to realize it. The more real the goal feels to your brain, the faster you'll achieve it.

If a goal is set far away; you wouldn't feel that it is realistic. You would find it difficult to have a sense of the goal world a reality. However, I am encouraging you to place your goals *outside of the status quo*. The world outside of the status quo is a world you have never seen before. I can tell you that it's hard to feel that this world is real.

It may sound contradictory, but we would like to devise a way to make it feel as real as possible, although it doesn't feel naturally real. What should we do? You need to create a realistic *picture*, *image*, and *feeling* with a combination of actual experiences.

To make it feel as real as possible you should combine the image of your future comfort zone with the memories of actual experiences. This is how the *100-time- growth* mindset works.

Also, if the goal is not realistic enough, management would easily make wrong decisions and judgments. In contrast, imagine someone, who has built a company with annual sales of 100 million dollars several times. He/she has already experienced *100-time growth* and will be able to deal with various aspects of management practices.

If this person starts a new business from scratch, he/she will run a company of 1 million dollars while knowing about the actual situation of a 100-million-dollar company. Surely, the quality of his/her decisions and judgments will be quite high. It will be very different from moving forward by trial and error.

Top management makes so many decisions every day. If it were 10 times a day, it would be thousands of times a year. If you include decisions made by employees, it will be a huge number. Whether the correctness of these judgments is in the 70th percentile or over the 90th percentile can make a big difference. If you think about it, you can understand the importance of increasing the sense of reality of the world of the goal.

## As long as you have a general direction, it will be fine

It is best if the goal is placed far away from the status quo. However, it doesn't have to be definite. You just need to have a general direction in place. Goal setting is setting a direction of *this is what I want to be*. If the direction is right, there is no problem. After that, you can just modify it as you go. It doesn't matter how much you modify the goal. You will improve your accuracy as you progress. There is no problem at all with this attitude.

However, even if "a general direction is established," there are certain goals that cannot be accepted. A typical example is setting goals that are not *want-to* goals. This is not a rare case. This is another example I often encounter.

Suppose a high school student says, "I want to study hard and become a medical doctor." This can also be one goal. Medicine is certainly a great profession. But, if I ask him/her "Why do you want to be a doctor?" and if the answer is "Because my father is an independent physician and I am expected to follow in his footsteps in the future," what do you think?

It's possible that after becoming a doctor, he/she may end up feeling "this is not what I imagined." Thus, it is quite common to assume that something that is not a *want-to* is a *have-to*.

Especially in the past generations in Japan, it was common for the breadwinner of the family to work 60 or more hours per week. However, it is conceivable that some people were fed up with this way of working, yet they needed to make a living. It is important to recognize your true feelings.

There is also the stereotypical thinking that "Work is for making a living. There is no question of like or dislike. To be able to realize the goals set for me, I need to suppress my feelings and contribute to the company. That's what adults do." People from that generation will have difficulty in switching to the *want-to* mindset.

One day when I was teaching at a university, a student from Eastern Europe said something like this to me. "I think the concept of *want-to* is great. However, I find it very difficult, perhaps because I grew up in the former communist world. My home country was democratized when I was 19 years old, and the landscape of society changed drastically. It would be acceptable to live in a *want-to* mindset now, but it's going to take quite a while before I can do so. I can't get rid of the memories of that time."

In some countries, it can be difficult to live a life based on a *want-to* mindset. It could be impractical because of differences in political conditions or national character. But even if you are from such a country, if I ask, "The truth is that you prefer *want-to*, don't you?" the answer is always "Yes."

It's been more than two decades since the 21st century began. In many countries, there is nothing wrong with *want-to*. It is fine. And what you must think of as a subset of *want-to* is *autonomy*. You need to think about how much you take responsibility for the outcome. There is no point in pursuing *want-to* so much that you end up with millions of dollars in debt and get stuck.

But if you still want to do it, you should go through with it. Even if it doesn't work out and you lose everything, you won't die of starvation that easily. It's an extreme argument, but we can manage it. If that's the case, wouldn't it be better to live your life doing what you want to do?

## Goal setting ➡ Taking action is the basic

Even if goals are set successfully, there is a trap that many people fall into. Even if you move forward following the theory, if you don't act, nothing will happen. It may seem obvious, but such cases are surprisingly common. It's common for people interested in self-development to read through the explanation of the Goal Theory and get satisfied with it. It doesn't lead to the next step of action from there. Many people buy and read a book on strategy or PDCA but won't go further from there. Many people don't act on it. So, let's make sure we do.

This book presents simple practices and exercises to make it easier to act. It's hard to start taking action if you make a big deal about it. It doesn't matter if it's a small thing, it is important to make a start. Little by little, you will be moving toward your goal. So, don't worry.

How can I be so sure? A small step may seem to be insignificant to you, but the human brain is designed to show us the path to reach the goal we have set for ourselves.[24]

---

24  Learn to trust your deep inner self. Editor

Therefore, that step will not be in vain. Just take the first step. Also, follow your intuition when taking a step. Give it a try. Then, you can go further by gathering momentum. All you must do is try first. Think about it later, do it first.

Here's what I would like you to do as a senior person. If a familiar face pops in your head and you think "I want to go out for a drink with him," give him a call. If you feel like stopping by somewhere on your way home, just do it. It may be a bookstore, a shopping mall, or a restaurant. I don't know where you feel like going but start walking there. When your mind moves a little, you turn your feet there. There may be nothing there. Even, if there is nothing, it's still a good idea to go there. Aren't you rejecting your own idea because "it's something I don't usually do?" It is often yourself who is holding you back in the status quo. Don't miss out on the chance to shift your comfort zone.

## Good visualization and bad visualization

There are good visualizations and bad visualizations for visualizing your future self. First of all, visualization will be more effective when it can be felt with all five senses, not just seen. Also, it is fine if the distant goal seems vague. The important thing is to look at it *from your own point of view*, which is an essential part of a highly realistic visualization. This may seem to be a trivial tip, but I point it out here.

Let's say you are visualizing your future self being interviewed. The image in your mind must be one that you see as the interviewee from your view. It cannot be an image broadcasted on television where you and the interviewer are sitting side by side. This is what I mean when I say that "your point of view" enhances the sense of reality.

Here's one effective exercise to help you reach your goals. Envision an ideal week 10 years from now. It is a kind of visualization, and it is meaningful that it is set as one week instead of one day because it includes days off.

One of the original methods that I have developed is *high-speed visualization.* The human sense of time is relative. You might have heard the story of how a person's whole life flashes in the mind just before death. I don't know if it's true or not, because there are not many people who have experienced it in the living world. However, when I hear this story, it seems true.

## High-speed visualization technique

Let's assume that humans can replay a long period of memory in a few seconds. Let's put this ability to work. Look 10 years ahead from now and try to play a week through your mind, in an hour. Then try to do the same in 15 minutes. As you practice you will be able to do this in a much shorter time. In the end, you will reduce this to 1 second. Memories are compressible.

You should keep visualizing this one second such that it will replay unconsciously all the time. I have mastered this skill so that I'm always reminiscing where I will be in 20 years. Now I can achieve my goals without writing a balance wheel.

Continue this visualization unconsciously for 24 hours a day. It will make an incredible difference to you if you do this.

## What if the organization's goals are different from your goals?

What should we do in a situation in which our own goals are not aligned with the goals of the organization we belong to? First, let's talk about the basic premise. It is only natural that the goals of the organization are different from the goals of the individuals who are part of it.

Having said that, there **is a balance wheel on both sides, so it should be possible** to find a point of commonality somewhere. You just need to be able to discover that point. If this point can be identified, the individuals will be happy, and the company will also benefit.

---

**Figure 7: Goals of organization and goals of individuals**

Organization and individuals have common goals at some levels of abstraction

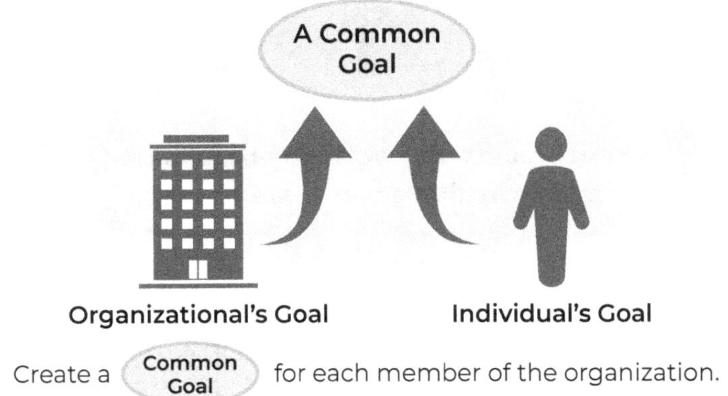


**Leaders need to create a goal that subsumes the goals of all the employees**

---

The key point here is to *not limit your goals to occupation*. When it comes to individuals, there are many reasons to work for an organization. Some say, "It's because I can demonstrate my expertise and abilities," others say "It's because it resonates with my philosophy," or "It's because the salary is good." Some might answer, "Because it's close to home," or "Because the working hours are flexible."

**Figure 8: What if the organization's goals seem to be different from your goals?**

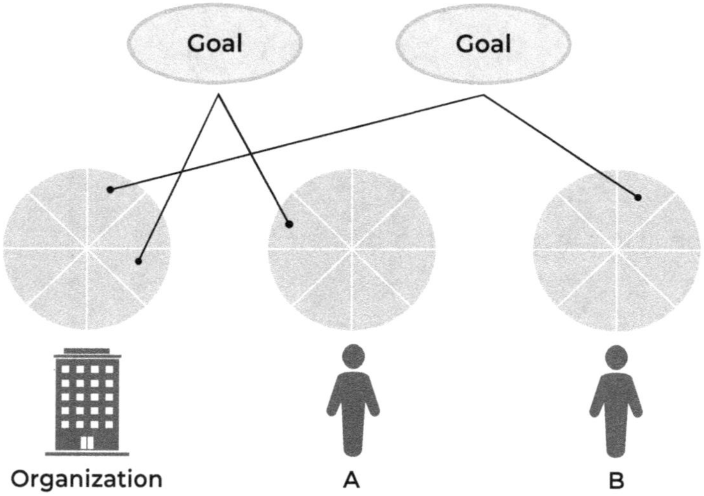

**Find a point that both an organization and individuals can share the goal**

Source: KAZUYOSHI HISANO AND CONOWAY, INC.

It's fine that there are a variety of motivations. The company needs to understand that as well. In this case, the company's side first refers to your immediate supervisor. Ideally, everyone should draw a balance wheel. If it's difficult, the supervisor, who is always looking at individual employees, can sense that he/she takes these points very seriously. If you can communicate in a way that considers personal goals or preferences, it will be more rewarding. Even if your organizational and personal goals are not aligned, you don't have to worry about it at all.

There is one more thing I would like the top management of the organization to be aware of. The goal should be high enough to be inclusive of all members' goals. The higher the goal is, the more likely it will be inclusive of everyone's goals. If top management just wants to "make money" as a goal, it will not be relevant to a majority of employees.

CHAPTER 3

## CHAPTER 3

# The Power to Believe in Yourself: Confidence

"If you don't believe in yourself,
you can't sustain your goals."

**Efficacy is a degree of self-evaluation that
you feel "I can achieve my goals"**

This is *the power to believe in yourself*. It is the confidence in your goals and abilities. It doesn't matter what position or title you hold. Efficacy is the confidence that you can reach your goals and realize your vision.

Efficacy is an enabler for the future. There's nothing wrong with using what you've done in the past to evaluate your ability to realize your goals in the future. However, if you say, "I am great because I have done this much in the past," what I can say is just, "That's right." If the sales representative achieved the top performance nationwide this year, that's great. But what if the achievement was about two or three years ago?

An evaluation of oneself from the past extrapolated to the present is called "self-esteem," and it can be translated as "self-respect." It is a sense of feeling that you are a valuable person. Self-esteem is based on what you did in the past. What you have done in the past is certainly important but just staying there will not generate anything. So long as the experience is used for self-evaluation of your ability to achieve your future goals, it will serve you well. In this sense, self-evaluation or self-esteem is part of the efficacy.

Now, let's talk about the goal. I have repeatedly pointed out the importance of setting a high goal. In many cases, if the goal is too high, you may think "I may not be able to do this," and the goal gradually goes down. It is efficacy that works to stop this declining trend. It supports you like a "trampoline." If your efficacy is high, you can keep your goals high.

Shout in your mind, "I can definitely achieve my goal." Now, the person next to you shouted in his/her mind as well. Did it bother you? No matter how high the person next to you held his or her efficacy to oneself, it did not affect you, right? The fact is, no matter how high your self-efficacy is, it would not bother anyone.

People are often surprised to hear this because our upbringing suggests that confidence is a form of *ego*, therefore it should not be admired. In my opinion, this kind of thinking is not correct.

Of course, you should not behave arrogantly to others because of excessively high self-evaluation. There is a big difference between behaving arrogantly and saying to yourself "I am great," and "I can do it." Unlike the former, there are only good things about the latter.

The most important thing in efficacy is *wholehearted certainty*. You just keep believing in your abilities.

## Humans talk to themselves
## 50,000 times a day (Self-talk)

It is said that people talk to themselves 50,000 times a day. Of course, it is not that someone strictly counted, but at least you can see that it's not at the level of a few hundred times a day.

The term, self-talk itself is not so uncommon. However, I divide the self-talk into two types *bubbling-up type* and *imprinting type*.

The *bubbling-up type* is something that comes out naturally. The *imprinting type* is what you tell yourself to do. The direction is the opposite. When you observe your self-talk, identify which type of self-talk it is.

So, what kind of self-talk is good? The answer is simple. Self-talk that brings you closer to your goals is good.

To put it simply, bad self-talk is something like "I'm not good enough," or "After all, I cannot do it anyway." This kind of talk won't get you any closer to your goal. If you find yourself doing this kind of self-talk often, try to gradually change your words with ones that will bring you closer to your goal.

Here, I want to make a distinction between "positive self-talk" and "negative self-talk."

Examples of the former are something like, "I can do this," "This is not like me," and "What shall I do next?" All of them are the words that bring out your true and positive self. The latter is "I am better (worse) than xx," "I could have done this before," "Why can't I do it?", etc.

The problem with "I am better (worse) than xx" and "I could have done this before" is that they are comparisons. And rather than digging into the reasons "why you can't do it," it will be more constructive to think about how you will do better next time.

To wrap up self-talk, let me give you a specific example. It is called an *affirmation*. Affirmations are a type of *imprinting type self-talk*. To ingrain the desired state in your mind you must use simple phrases such as "I am great" in your self-talk. The point is to say it with certainty and tell yourself several times a day.[25]

Free yourself from the three constraints; "time," "other people," and "money"

---

[25] When I was 35, I was afraid of flying and afraid of heights. In the Army, I walked around every obstacle, (I just couldn't climb them.) Luckily, I didn't get caught or I would have spent at least one week in the "brig". Magically, years later, I was taught to "chant" some words to myself over and over again and within one month all my fears disappeared. – Editor

It's not easy to improve your efficacy by yourself. On the other hand, it's easy to lower it. There are many factors that can lower your efficacy, but there are three that are hard to notice because they are so deeply woven into our daily lives. I refer to these as the *three scales or three standards*. They are *time*, *other people*, and *money*. Although I use the word *scale* for convenience, it actually is *conditioning*.

The most powerful of these is *money*. Money is certainly important in the world of capitalism. However, if you assume that you are great because you have money, or not because you don't, it will be extremely difficult to live and nurture future-oriented thinking.

Money is an important tool. However, thinking that "I can't do it because I don't have the money" is not the way that should be. Rather, we should think "I don't have money now, but what do I need to do to achieve my goal?"

First, let's free ourselves from the complexity of money. An easy and effective way to do this is to "tear up a 100-dollar bill." This is a rite of passage to experience that *a bank bill is just a piece of paper*. I wish there was another easy way to do it, but for now, this is the simplest.

It might be a good idea to try living without any money at all. If you experience that you can get by without money, you will realize that money is just a useful tool.

Just to confirm, money, which is paper, has no value in and of itself. Let's say you paid hundreds of dollars to eat "sushi." What is of real value is not in the ingredients themselves but in the presence and activities of the fishermen, farmers, chefs, and carpenters who built the restaurants, etc. It is human beings themselves and their activities that create value.

Let's say you meet a person who is what people consider rich, a wealthy person or a millionaire. If you are subconsciously intimidated, it is a sign that money has you in its power.

A client of mine tore up a 100-dollar bill, framed it, and hung it in his room. By looking at it every day and thinking, "This is paper," he is freeing himself from the kind of worship of money.

When you're free from the thrall or power of money controlling you, strangely you will be able to make more money. I'm not saying that tearing up a 100-dollar bill is mandatory, but when you can say, "This is paper," unexpected things start to happen.

If you met someone with the ability to "drink a lot of water," would you be intimidated and say, "He is amazing?" Making a lot of money or drinking a lot of water, there is no intrinsic difference between the two. But the reality is that only the former is particularly appreciated.

It is not that money is great. All you require is what you need. You are free to decide how much you need. If money is a prerequisite for your goal, then earn it. If not, you don't have to earn that much.

## Once you envision the future, the future will come to you

When we try to set high goals, we find it difficult to achieve them if we think that time flows from the past to the present and from the present to the future. Some kind of excuses might pop up in your mind, and like "Well…but …" may come out of your mouth.

Let's flip the idea around. How about thinking that time is flowing from the future to the present? That should make better sense.

What does it mean by making better sense? Successful and accomplished people have this kind of mindset. "When you envision a future, that future manifests itself and then that present reality becomes the past."

For example, let's say you want to do something next weekend. You make a plan, the weekend comes, the planned things are done, and it is over. You would not feel anything strange about this sequence. It is quite natural. This is what I mean when I say, "When you decide on a future, that future comes and becomes the present, and then that present becomes the past."

You will only do something if you decide to do it. By repeating "Decide and make it happen," your ability to work on the future will be enhanced. Of course, you are free to think and say, "This is how it was in the past, so this is how it will be in the future." But isn't it more fun and empowering to make your own decisions for your future?

Even though I have explained this so far, I think many of you are still thinking, "This is how I have always been." I want to turn this "common sense" upside down. That's what I want.

When you strengthen your future-oriented thinking and increase your efficacy, you'll be able to set higher goals.

Successful people always think "I can do this." As long as you think, "I have a dream, but it's probably impossible," it won't come true. Of course, even if you don't fully believe in yourself, there will be flukes from time to time. But it will not last long.

On the contrary, I am sometimes asked "If I believe in myself, can I always achieve my goals?" Of course not. However, if you believe in yourself and work on it, at least you will be closer to your goal than where you are now. There can be no doubt about this.

## How to improve your power to believe in yourself

You need four elements to enhance your efficacy.

## 1. Have a high goal (power to see the future).

By setting high goals, you will be able to think, "It's awesome that I have high goals and am trying to achieve them." There is a question of which comes first, chicken (goal) or egg (efficacy), but I can assure you that it works.

# 2. Surround yourself with good people (power to involve and move people).

"Good people" in this case are those who have a high self-image. In other words, those with high efficacy. When you share the space where such people gather, your own efficacy will also increase. You can look at the behaviors and habits of people you admire and incorporate them into yourself.

# 3. Shift your viewpoint to the future (feedforward).

The longer the timeline, the easier it is to believe in your potential.

# 4. Positive self-talk.

*Positive words* are those that allow you to develop your potential. Positive self-talk increases your efficacy.

In addition to this, it is also essential to be free from the three scales, which were already mentioned, *money, time,* and *other people.* I have explained about money in detail. The scale of time means that you get trapped in the past. I talked about this a few times as well. So, what is the scale of other people? This is the "attitude of worrying about the opinion of others." To be free from other people's scale means "stop worrying about other people's opinions and have your own opinion of yourself."

Having said that, there may be people who are concerned about other people's viewpoints. Then, look at your goals. No matter what kind of noise comes in from around you, you will not waver if you have a clear direction to go.

## How to deal with the negative feelings

No matter how much you enhance your efficacy, you can't be completely positive. Still, negative emotions may arise. Here, let me explain how to deal with such cases.

The first step is to savor the negativity that comes up. It is okay to be depressed. It is fine to cry too. After tasting it, write down your feelings as they are. For the sake of your brain, you should write it by hand, if possible, but you can also use your smartphone's note function.

Write down "I'm depressed right now." "I'm now immersed in a feeling of sadness." Writing helps you to accept your emotions with an objective view. As a result, you will be able to calm down.

Eventually, looking at what you wrote, you will recognize that "I'm sad (disappointed, angry, etc.) right now." Once you come this far, you should be able to detach yourself from your emotions. It may continue to go around in your head. If you feel better for a moment and then the negative thoughts come back five minutes later, repeat the process.

Gradually, the intervals will increase, and you can forget them eventually. In my opinion, you should not suppress the emotions that are coming up. There is no point in forcing them to stop. You need to listen to the voice of your mind unless you have an urgent job or an errand to run. In such cases, put a lid on your feelings for the moment, and finish your errands.

## Affirmations that work on the roots of the mind

The affirmations I mentioned earlier have a slightly more advanced way of application.

I have already explained that making your "to be" affirmation can be highly effective. Making affirmations such as "I am an excellent manager" is one example.

Let's take it a step further and incorporate affirmations about your true nature. It can strengthen your inner self. "I am a cheerful person." "I am an honest person." "I am a kind person." Say those words. The person who can say "I am a cheerful person" in the first place is already a cheerful person. Putting it into words further strengthens the roots.

It is also important to know "where to put the affirmations." Think of what it's like to grow a flower bulb. You can treat your affirmation like fertilizer for the flower. There seem to be two ways to fertilize it:

One way is to lift the plant with a shovel and put the fertilizer in the deepest place near the roots. Another way is to put fertilizer on the surface expecting that the nutrition goes down from there.

The way affirmations are made is like this. You should put the "affirmations about your nature" at the deepest level. And "affirmations of what you want to be" may be placed in a shallower place than that.

By the way, I once set a goal of "being the kindest person in the world" and did the affirmation "I am the kindest person in the world." I think I have accomplished this goal. I am now continuing my affirmations toward my goal of "being the kindest person in the universe." I feel that I am getting closer to the goal every day.

## When other people's self-talk bothers you

Sometimes we hear other people's self-talk. If the content is negative, listening to it will lower your efficacy. How should we deal with this? Try not to listen. This is a basic solution. There will be many ways to do this. You can put on earplugs or walk away from the self-talk. Of course, it would also be a good idea to reach out to the person doing the negative self-talk to help them increase their "levels of futurism" or "levels of abstraction."

For example, your acquaintance has a serious illness and is fighting against it. Although he has not yet been told how much he has time remaining to live, he sometimes says, "I don't have much time left." There is no point in agreeing with what he says but try to empathize with him by saying, "I see," and "I hear you." After a while, you may suggest to him about the future, such as "Where should we go on our next trip?"

Eventually, the topic of "limited time left" will be averted and forgotten.[26] It doesn't do any good to keep talking

---

26  I wish I knew this earlier. I was teaching at a retirement home, when I looked at a very sad old man who said to me, "I am dying." I didn't know what to say to him. I only thought that "everyone is dying," especially at an old age home. – Editor

about how much longer he can live. This is an example of a conversation that increases the levels of futurism.

Next, let's talk about how to increase the levels of abstraction. Inside the company, executives are talking about a high-performing employee who has submitted a resignation letter. A human resources director says, "If we hold him back now, it could have a negative effect. Shall we hire a new person? What kind of person would be good? How about someone who can work abroad? How about a person with foreign language skills?" The key is to speak without making it obvious that you intend to urge others to increase the levels of abstraction.

You may hear the positive self-talk of others as well. In this case, you should get involved in the talk. "It's great that you are positive!" "You are amazing!" This kind of encouragement will help you stay positive as well.

## Spend time with "people who believe in themselves"

People who "believe in themselves" have a high comfort zone. They can use that power to enhance their efficacy. If you spend time with those who believe in themselves and whose comfort zone is high, you will learn how to use your brain similarly.

Ideally, put yourself where only people with high comfort zones gather. Surrounding yourself with them will significantly improve your efficacy. In my experience, I found that people with a high comfort zone have common thoughts and physical traits:

1. First, what they say is positive. From an average person's perspective, they may sound more optimistic than they need to be. They are only interested in "how to get through" even in difficult situations. They put the cause analysis aside for the time being and suggest, "Anyway, let's think about how to get over this."

2. In terms of appearance, they tend to have a good posture, erect and forward-looking. The gait is relatively slow. At least they wouldn't rush around. They are usually smiling and breathing deeply. They always look like they are having fun. And most of all, they are in high spirits.

3. Their motto is "Let's just do it." And they don't do what they don't want to. They seem to avoid it as much as possible. They may still do something they are not willing to do, but they never let it linger with them. They shift their emotional gears quickly.

4. They openly talk about their dissatisfaction with the status quo, but don't speak ill of others. Talking about dissatisfaction does not mean they complain, rather they make suggestions for improvement. They can see the gap between the to-be state and the current state, so they calmly present issues and solutions.

## Write down 10 or more success stories, and you'll believe in yourself

The *power to believe in yourself* is basically the ability to believe in your future self. Past successes are not always relevant to the future. On the contrary, if you are stuck in the past, your ability to move forward will be weakened. However, there are exceptions. You can use your past successful experiences to help you believe in your future self.

What is important here is to only utilize the *emotions* of the moment. The key point is not to go into the past events themselves, but to re-live only the emotions.

An experience, even if it is a successful one, contains many judgments and actions that were done in "the comfort zone at that time." Those judgments and actions belong to the past. They often don't fit the comfort zone of the future. Therefore, extract only the *emotions*, and forget other details.

Even if you were once the top salesperson, thinking about the image of receiving the award does not lead to the future. Don't go back to what you were then. Rather, only extract the past emotions at the time. Writing some of those past emotions down is quite effective for enhancing efficacy.

## The importance of distracting yourself from the "things you couldn't do"

How should we deal with failures in keeping our efficacy high? In the first place, you can't even call it a failure if it's something you couldn't do only once or twice. If you want to continue something, keep trying. The game isn't over yet. The important thing is what you are going to do about it from now.

A somber person more likely tends to analyze the cause wondering "Why couldn't I do it?" This behavior itself is not a problem. However, you should not forget that it is a lesson to be used for the future. If the analysis itself becomes an objective, it will get you nowhere.

From the perspective of how the brain works, it is advisable to distance yourself from what you couldn't do in the past. Just focusing on "something you couldn't do" doesn't make you capable of doing it. When you start to think that you are capable of doing it, the situation will turn around in time. The analysis will mostly reveal something obvious.

## When you cannot find an answer, try changing your environment

Sometimes it may be hard to find the answer. In such cases, I recommend you change your environment. When you spend your days in a fixed comfort zone, new ideas are hard to come up. By changing the environment, which is easy to do, you may see what you didn't see. It doesn't have to be a big change. Even if you try something small, it will make a difference.

The next thing I would like you to do is to challenge yourself, to constantly do something a little difficult. It's important to keep your comfort zone moving, even little by little. In order to do so, try to incorporate various challenges of all types, including big ones and small ones, into your work and life. If your every day is filled with varieties of challenges, big and small, the movement of your comfort zone will gradually accelerate.

## Everyone has a "zone where he/she can believe in oneself" (confidence zone)

Anyone who can "believe in themselves," (confidence area) can exert their power in a sphere of influence. So, if you want to exercise your ability, it's important to make the area of your fight into your comfort zone. Whether you fight in your comfort zone or make the place you fight a part of your comfort zone, you need to think strategically. To do this, *goal setting* is important, and the Balance Wheel can be used. Once you become familiar with the process, you can expect to become the person who easily gets high performance.

For example, if you're going to do something new, go to the place to look it over beforehand. Do so not just once but several times. If you are going to give a speech at a wedding reception, try standing in the hall. It may be a small thing, but not so many people actually do this. The results will be very different. The more you practice, the better your performance will be. There is no person who cannot do it. It is you who decides whether you can or can't do it. Let's expand the area where you can think "I can do it."

**CHAPTER 4**

# The Power to Involve and Move People: Involvement

---

**Successful people place themselves
in a new comfort zone**

There are certainly necessary things to achieve great success. Probably, the first thing is to recognize that you are living in a *comfort zone*[27] you have created for yourself so far and that it may not be suitable for what you want in the future.

---

27  A comfort zone is a place or state where the unconscious feels comfortable.

To be successful, you need to establish a new high goal that will take you into a new *comfort zone*, which at first might not be comfortable at all. But, by unswervingly believing in yourself, you will surely attain success.

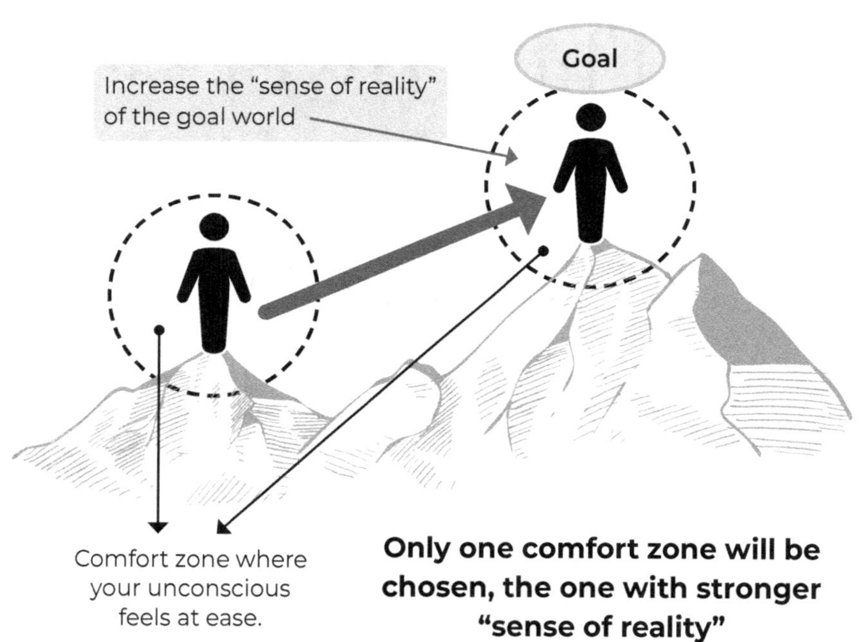



### So, what determines the comfort zone?

It is the people you engage with and spend time with that determines your comfort zone. For example, suppose one day, ten million dollars is suddenly deposited into your bank account. Will your life be different the following day? If you didn't realize that money was deposited into your account, you will live the same life without any change. Of course, you'll notice it when you update your bankbook, but it shouldn't change your life that much. Some people may be concerned that they have fallen for some kind of scam.

---

## Comfort Zone

- Comfort zone is the physical or psychological area of tolerance within which you feel comfortable and at ease.
- Inside it is everything you've done often enough to feel confident about. It encompasses all your ideas and images of who you are and what you're like, where you belong, how you live, with whom you associate, etc.
- Inside of the comfort zone is the collection of information that passed RAS.
- Outside of the comfort zone is scotoma.

**You can decide your comfort zone by setting your own goal.**

Reference: Personal Coaching for Result

---

So, at what point does your life begin to change? Does the change begin when you spend that new money and make a big purchase? I think the answer is "No."

Just having fun shopping doesn't change your comfort zone. Your comfort zone really starts to change when you start to spend that money and interact with those people that you perceive are richer and more successful. The new perception might be triggered when you join the wine circle and start to taste and enjoy expensive wines. Or when you start joining a membership-only golf or sports club and spend time with the members there. When you start spending more time with wealthy people, your comfort zone starts to shift in that direction.

Your comfort zone is made up of a variety of experiences and elements, and it's largely influenced by what kind of people you spend your time with. Even if you spend ten million dollars just to satisfy your desires, your comfort zone will only slightly shift. However, there is a way to make it work even better. That is to get more people involved. As a result, with the help of others, your comfort zone will shift to a higher dimension.

## Housewife who turned a ten-million-dollar stock into a scrap of paper

One of my staff members who helped me publish this book bought a stock for ten thousand dollars before it went public. It just so happened that her husband was an acquaintance of the owner of the company. After listing, her holdings became worth close to ten million dollars. She tried to sell the stock at its peak price, but her husband stopped her. He said, "These stocks were given to me by the president who has been so supportive. You can't sell them at this time." However, after the collapse of the Murakami Fund, the share price dropped to a tenth of its value, and then to a further tenth of its value with the subsequent Lehman Brothers crisis. Eventually, the company was delisted, and the stock turned effectively into wastepaper.

During that time, her life didn't change at all. Her comfort zone was modest in a good way, but if she had started a business with the help of a brilliant business partner or investor when she had the ten million dollars, she could have changed her entire world.

In her case, she didn't have someone to help manage her assets, or a coach to give her financial advice. Because she had no clear goal, she lost a valuable asset. She couldn't take advantage of that chance to shift her comfort zone.

As this example shows, *continuing the status quo* doesn't change your life. A mistake in choosing to *do nothing* can lead to a significant loss of wealth.

In all ages and countries, I believe, a company that becomes defensive inevitably falls into decline. To prevent this from happening, it is important to be mindful of shifting the comfort zone and making connections that can lift you from the status quo.

## There's only so much you can do on your own

There is only so much you can do on your own – that's right. Let us look at the present times and environment. With the evolution of technology, it is now possible for a person to do quite a few things with the help of tools such as the Internet. The problem, though, is that your comfort zone is unlikely to change if you just keep doing things by yourself. Without changing your comfort zone, you might end up not growing at all.

Therefore, we recommend you strive to put yourself amid people, who may have other talents to help you. The *amid people,* in this case, does not necessarily mean that it must always be a real environment. You can make great use of virtual space, like Zoom.

Information comes to you from many kinds of people. Primary information can only come from a relationship of trust. In particular, the most important thing is whether others feel you are trustworthy.

There are a lot of things you cannot do without information. In today's world of convenience, we must keep in mind that the core of business is building and maintaining relationships of trust.

I have a friend who got interested in motorsports. He was always an excellent and enthusiastic mechanic who often visited the racing circuit. I used to say to him "If you like it so much, why don't you do it?"; but he couldn't take the plunge.

However, one day, he took a small step in the motorsport world. At first, he started slowly and tentatively, but eventually, he began to fit in with others who had advanced their career. He gradually became a resident of that comfort zone. It seems to have costed a lot of money, but it's what he wanted to do in the first place. He transformed into his *new self.* He was the president of a company, and his involvement in motorsports led him to a new business too. He wasn't expecting that to happen at the beginning, but he is pleased with this outcome, saying "When the comfort zone changes, it changes the world."

## The four powers to gain trust and support

Let's review the basic premise of the comfort zone again. The comfort zone is made up of *people*. The key to *Gold Vision* is the transition to a new comfort zone. Therefore, what kind of people are around you is important.

Here are *four powers to gain trust and support* that will help you become a person who shares a place with people who are attractive and powerful.

## 1. The power to encounter:
### Where and who do you meet?

One contact in the world you want to go to outweighs 100 acquaintances in the place where you are now. To develop this power, it is essential to have a good goal set.

### Figure 9: The Power to Connect

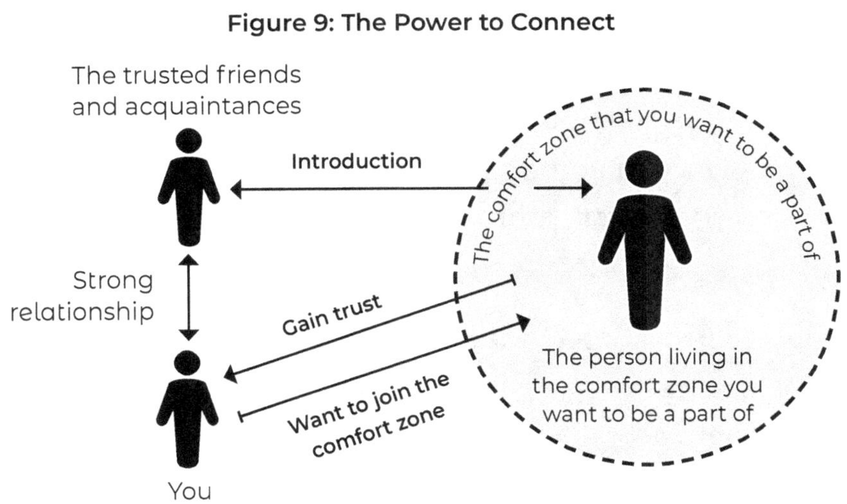


Source: KAZUYOSHI HISANO AND CONOWAY, INC.

## 2. The power to connect:
### How do you move to a new place?

Comfort zones are made up of people. If so, then the greatest gift is connecting people. Introduce someone you know who would be appreciated by the residents in the comfort zone you want to move into; that will dramatically increase their confidence in you. Of course, referrals should not be based on your egoistic motivation. It is important to create a connecting opportunity that your acquaintance will also appreciate.

## 3. The power to be trusted:
### How do others view you?

Your efficacy level (your ability to believe in yourself) is very important. For that, you need to be working with a want-to mindset.

## 4. The power to be recommended:
### Can you come up with a one-word tag or
### a short phrase to describe you?

You need this one-word or phrase tag that describes and helps you in your new comfort zone. You can have many tags. The tag preferably should express the role you are playing in the comfort zone you want to shift to, rather than the one that you are in now.

Luffy, a Japanese cartoon character defines himself as "I'm the man who's going to be the pirate king." This is exactly the expression of the role that he is playing in the comfort zone where he will go to. It is an ideal tag. In another cartoon, Shin calls himself "the man who will become a great general in the world." This is also a pretty good tag.

I use a few tags for myself such as "CEO coaching" and "0.3 second coaching." What is your tag?[28]

**Figure 10: The Power to be Recommended**

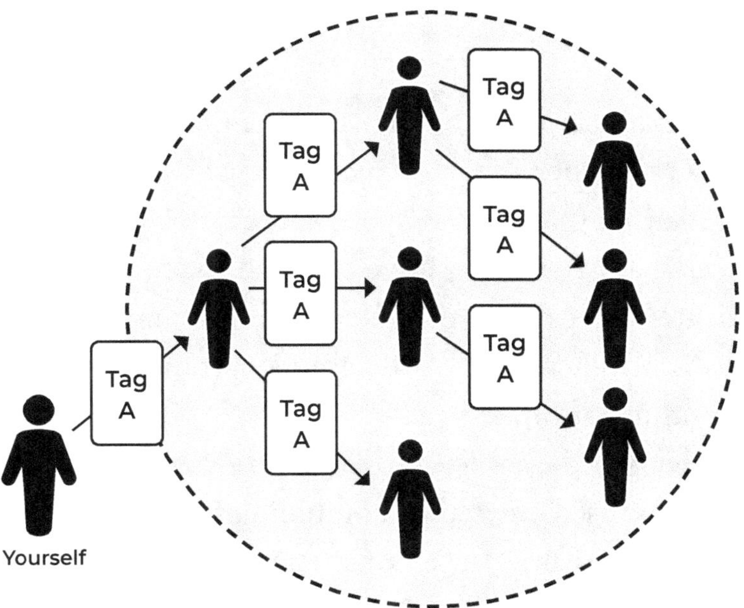


**Your tag will circulate in the new comfort zone**

Source: KAZUYOSHI HISANO AND CONOWAY, INC.

28  My tag is "discoverer of great talent." Magically, I have found many management masters, especially in Japan, published their books in English and brought their brilliance to the Western World. – Editor

## The three powers for aligning people with your vision

Once you successfully become established in the new comfort zone, it's time to start communicating your goals to the people around you. What is necessary here is to strengthen *the power to align people with your vision*. There are three powers to make your vision resonate with others:

### 1. The power to communicate:
Rather than what you talk about, what is important is the kind of person you are.

---

Your subconscious thought is transmitted. Information that has a higher sense of reality can be communicated easily. Rather than refining your speech, it is wiser to refine yourself with the perspective that the subconscious communicates more eloquently. Keep in mind that the subconscious is primary, and words are a complimentary means of communication.

In other words, *the levels of authenticity* are transmitted. This is a phrase I created by combining the five concepts of "levels of futurism," "levels of abstraction," "distance from the status quo," "strength of the cause," and "altitude of the cause." What you're aiming for (the goal) and what you believe in (the cause) will come across through your subconscious—therefore, your maturity as an individual is important.

## 2. The power to implant:
### Communication that can make people naturally want to support you.

---

People get serious normally when they decide to do things by themselves. How do other people decide to support you? The key is whether they have enough information about you and your goals. For this, you need to provide sufficient information about yourself and your goals at regular intervals to plant ideas into them. When you do this, the other person's subconscious mind creates a story and helps them weave it into their perspective of the world. It is necessary to let them persuade themselves into a state of self-conviction, not pushing them.

## 3. The power to nurture:
### Be caring to be remembered.

---

Since you will deliver information intermittently, you will need to remind people, so they don't forget you. We live in an age where there's a lot of information, so it's important to create a system for people to remember you.

### Get the principle of homeostasis[29] on your side

*Homeostasis* or *homeostatic mechanism* is a characteristic of a living creature that tries to keep its internal environment

---

29 Homeostasis, any self-regulating process by which biological systems tend to maintain stability while adjusting to conditions that are optimal for survival. – Encyclopedia Britannica

in a constant state. Homeostasis is, in other words, a comfort zone. You need to aggregate all your thoughts and activities so that you are automatically drawn into the comfort zone that you want to move into. This is done by setting a high goal. The center of the comfort zone you want to move to is the goal. That's the place that you will be automatically drawn into.

The important thing here is to trust your intuition[30]. If you can't do this, you may not be able to get there even if you know the answer. It is said that if a rocket can't reach the critical velocity, it won't be able to break through the atmosphere, and it will be pulled back to the earth. It's the same thing here. If you don't reach out fully to the new comfort zone using a strong goal, you will be pulled back to where you are. You need speed and power to shift into the new comfort zone. Otherwise, the gravitational pull of the old status quo will ensure that you stay where you are. Your goal gives you the new force to break out.

## The "Power of Others" – people who don't get supported will never succeed

I think a lot of people were taught from their childhood to be able to do things on their own. But what we really need is the ability to gather the support of others, *the power of*

---

30   Intuition is the ability to understand something instinctively, without the need for conscious reasoning. To me intuition is almost mystical when ideas come into my head seemly from outer space as opposed to coming from my mind. To me intuition is truth while often my thoughts are not. – Editor

*others*.[31] It is this that enables you to get help from others when it is required.

No matter what the path may be, there will always be someone who is ahead of you. You need to be the kind of person who can be assisted by those people. For this to happen, your goal and cause must be clear. Also, you must be the kind of person who will be able to help others. Those who help their juniors are often presented with more opportunities.

Here are a few traits seen in people who are less likely to be supported. First, people who are not trusted or credible will not be supported. People who only think of themselves will struggle to gain support.

People who easily draw support understand the importance of being supported. They work diligently to become the person whom others are likely to help. They live a life worthy of support.

On the other hand, people who feel that they do not need any help will downplay that need. As long as you think "If I work hard enough, I can make it work," you won't get a hand from those around you. Some people may not be able to admit their weaknesses. So, they just must work hard on their own.[32]

---

31 We live in a myth that we are "rugged individuals." Yes, in the 1700s and 1800s when we roamed the Wild West, we might have been that "rugged individual," but today we need each other to be successful. Don't be fooled by that term anymore – there are others like it to dominate by keeping you separate. – Editor

32 When in my thirties, I played golf probably twice a week even though I could not hit the ball straight. I did not take lessons thinking I should be able to learn this on my own. Finally, after playing eight holes and losing nine balls, I just threw the golf clubs away. A decade later, I met John Schlee, a professional golfer, who took me to the golf range, spent one hour coaching me and afterwards every ball went straight. In retrospect, I felt very foolish and learned a great lesson. - Editor

It's not so difficult to acquire *the power of others*. If you understand the importance of being supported, anyone can enhance the power in a short time. To gain cooperation and support from others, there are ways to respect their self-esteem. For example, name a new project after a person in your group and give them credit for the outcome. It's a bit technical, but the effect is powerful. By turning into the kind of person who is supported by others, you can step into a different dimension.

## A story about an emotional dream

Everyone wants to dream big about their company in the business world. This is especially true for the new millennials.

The most important thing to do is to envision the future vividly and emotionally. Share that feeling and increase the appeal (or attractiveness) of your organization. Of course, you can't ignore the numbers, but put them aside for the time being.

Cherish the time you spend sharing your big dreams. It's also a good idea to include a sense of togetherness, such as "Let's all go on a trip together when we achieve this." Many companies actually do so. Over time, these dreams get adopted across departments and divisions, and in some cases, even by higher-level business divisions and companywide.

## You can ignite motivation by empathizing with your employees' life goals

The life goals of each employee are different. This is natural. Show interest in those different goals and objectives. This is an essential quality for management, administrative executives, and leaders. Many employees don't expect their organization to be sensitive to an individual's dreams. Therefore, they feel very happy just to have their dreams acknowledged. If you do acknowledge them, you will see their motivation increase.

The challenge is to align the organizational goals with the individual employee's goals. Most executives want their people to align their goals with the company's goals, but we think differently.

We recommend that managers meet with employees to find out what they want and then see how the corporation and individual can find a point where both can align. This is very important. Even if you find it hard to empathize with an employee's life goals in an area you don't know much about, just accept it by saying, "So that's what you're interested in." You don't necessarily need a deep understanding of it. Just listening to them is fine. Employees who are listened to feel "I was acknowledged" and "this is where I belong." A change begins to occur unconsciously. Let's not stop that flow and continue to listen to their stories.[33]

---

33 Wow, just imagine how this world can change! Many companies have been run by command and control, but this is slowly changing. The "old boss," who thrived on keeping their employees living in "fear," is dying out. The new boss will know that their job is to bring out the best from people. "Let the dinosaurs disappear." – Editor

What if the company's goals and their personal goals appear different? They shouldn't be completely contradictory if you compare the balance wheels of the company and the individual. There will be a common point where you can get a grip somewhere. As long as the person belongs to the company, you should talk to them face to face. In rare occasions where you can't find common ground, you might have no choice but to take a different path.

**CHAPTER 5**

# The Power to Lead into the Future: Feedforward

"To enhance the levels of futurism means to
put your consciousness in the future."

Almost every company around the world does marketing when they create a new product. Marketing in this case refers to market research, product development, and advertising. They conduct research on consumers by asking "What products do you want now?" or "What's bothering you?" and develop products based on the consumers' needs, make advertising plans, and execute them. More than 99% of companies use this method.

However, there is one innovator who put "a dent in the universe" without doing any market research at all. That was Steve Jobs of Apple. He told everyone to "Think differently" and seriously tried to change the world. Without relying on market research, he created and released innovative products such as the iMac, iPod, iTunes, iPhone, and iPad that surprised everyone, based solely on his intuition. Is Jobs an exceptional genius?

Companies all over the world are looking at data from the past and using it to create future products and services. However, that's just an *optimization of the status quo*. It's a backward-looking stance on business.

This is because no matter how much you analyze customer preferences and insights; you will only create products and services that satisfy customers in the present based on past data. You can't always predict the future based on what happened in the past. No one knows what is going to happen in the future.

Evidence of this is the unpredictable growth taking place in information technology. A product or service that no one had thought of can become an explosive hit. You can't be bound by past data alone.

It is often said, "You should reflect on things from the past but look toward the future." However, we say, "First look at the future and then reflect," as we consider reflection to occur during the process of creating the future. Reflecting on the past first, and then moving on to the future is doing things in the wrong order.

Coaching helps you put it in the right order and predict the future. Coaching intends to solve problems in the future. It's a bit of a problem if a coach encourages you to reflect on the past. This is because the client will be tied to their past comfort zone. From a cognitive science perspective, the direction would be wrong.

For my clients to overcome the tendency to get caught up in the past, I always ask them *big questions* that help them get unstuck. The questions are like "What do you want to do from now on?" I don't ask "What do you want to do with your company?", or "How do you want to be by when?" I don't mention subject or objective pronouns. I omit those words as much as possible so that they will turn their thoughts toward their future without limitation. Many managers are then able to move away from the constraints of the past and envision their dreams for the future.

Any answer is fine. At the moment when the answer is uttered from the mouth of him/her, the brain begins to think about strategies, tactics, and methods to make that dream come true.

"What do you want your future to be like?" Ask yourself this question as many times as you want during every day. The new marketing lies in the future, not in the past.

With just one mobile device, Steve Jobs changed human lifestyles and transformed the world. What I admire most about Jobs is his imagination. He could see a future that no one else had ever seen before.

## The weakness of feedback lies in past-oriented thinking

Let me recap the framework of *Feedforward*. The brain cannot recognize two things at the same time. When you place your consciousness on the future, the significance of the past becomes weaker. No matter how much you look at the past, it is very difficult to create the future.

In general, people aren't satisfied with their past. They are often thinking, "Couldn't I have done it better?" When you look at the past, your energy is lowered.

It's been said since ancient times that "the best medicine to get over lost love is to start a new romance." This also expresses the spirit of Feedforward. By looking ahead instead of clinging to the past, you will feel better.

People take similar actions in their daily lives without even realizing it. In the world of Feedforward, we do this even more proactively. The value of the Feedforward will be clearer when it is compared to feedback. Let's think about the weaknesses of feedback.

Feedback focuses on events of the past and inevitably, you will fall into past-oriented thinking. You can't "feed-back on the future." This is a serious situation. As soon as the word "feedback" is mentioned, people will get into past-oriented thinking. Thus, to elicit future-oriented think-ing, I came up with *Feedforward*. Of course, it's important to learn something from the past and use it in the future. Looking at the past itself is not a bad thing. The problem is when you get caught up in the past, the ability to look into the future is diminished.

## Why is the PDCA difficult?[34]

**Figure 11: PDCA Cycle**

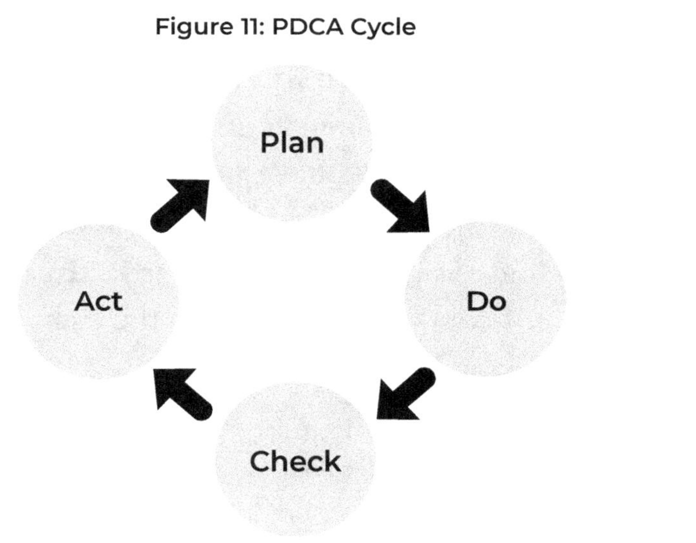


Source: Feedforward Thinking: Create The Future You Want (PCS Press) P.31

PDCA can be a very effective method to solve problems, but it has a different view from Feedforward. "PDCA" (Plan, Do, Check, and Act or Adjust). It is said that by repeating the four phases, P→D→C→A→P..., you can increase the efficiency of work. From the perspective of Feedforward, the P and C of the four phases are done based on the assumption of looking to the past. That is, PDCA is structured to bind a person to the past in half of the cycle.

The important parts of PDCA are D and A. If you don't take action, nothing will happen. However, for the reasons already mentioned, the PDCA cycle contains factors that

---

34  The PDCA approach was pioneered by Dr. William Deming.

sometimes make it difficult to act. To use a metaphor, it is like you're running with your weight shifted backward.

I am not completely denying the value of the PDCA cycle. However, only using PDCA will not be as effective to improve management. Feedforward contains the concept of "Feedforward Action." I recommend that you use it separately from the PDCA cycle. PDCA can be said to be a method for optimizing the past and the current situation. On the contrary, Gold Vision and Feedforward exist to *optimize the future*. Of course, we do look at the past, but we are primarily looking at the future.

**Figure 12: Long-term Feedforward Action Process**

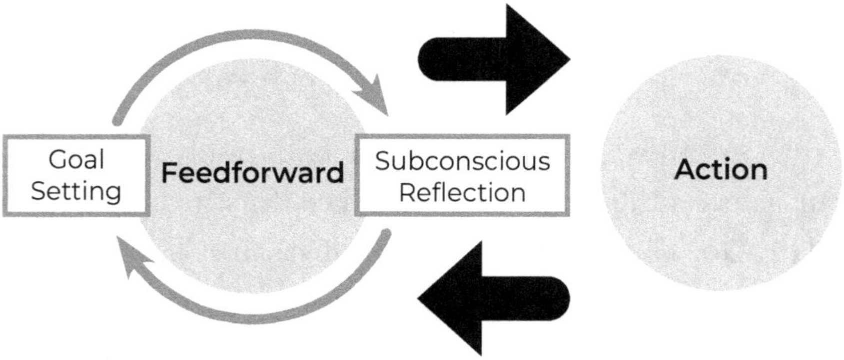

**"Feedforward" includes "Goal setting" and "Unconscious reflection"**

Source: Feedforward Thinking: Create The Future You Want (PCS Press) P.38

Depending on the industry or occupation, PDCA may be necessary. However, even in that case, having a Feedforward Action perspective can accelerate the improvement.

Feedforward Action will be indispensable in the field where more creative thoughts and actions are required. By intentionally using the term Feedforward Action, you can notice how it's working in your business.

Feedforward Action has another feature. Unlike PDCA, it has a deep trust in the subconscious. In PDCA, there is no trust in the subconscious. It is a method that is consciously executed. Because we trust the subconscious, there are only two stages in the Feedforward Action: Feedforward and Action. You may wonder "Will this really work?" Don't worry. It will work well.

I think we all lived in Feedforward Action when we were children. As we grow up, we unconsciously begin to tie ourselves down. Feedforward is also a method that is highly compatible with "*one-to-100* management" where intuition is utilized. Again, there are times when PDCA is necessary. However, there is a tendency for it to be emphasized too much. There is no "one size fits all" solution. You can maximize the effect by using these tools differently in different environments, situations, and applications.

Modern society is said to be *the age of VUCA*. VUCA is an acronym for the four keywords: *volatility*, *uncertainty*, *complexity*, and *ambiguity*. This acronym depicts a time of great volatility. You can't keep up with the flow of change by simply optimizing the past or the current situation. I want the *one-to-100* managers or *one-to-100* leaders to develop a sense of Feedforward Action.

## The first effect of Feedforward is to help others look to the future

I am going to talk about the two effects of Feedforward. The first one is *to help others look to the future*. In the Feedforward framework, we call the person who asks questions, like "What do you want to do from now on?" a *feedforwarder*, a *forwarder* for short, and the person who answers the question is called a *receiver*. The role of the forwarder is to help the receiver look to the future.

Receivers feel happy in being feedforwarded. They are pleased that others pay attention to them and take an interest in their future. For example, if you were asked "What are you going to do next weekend?" It pleases you to think the other person is caring about you, even if it is such a simple question. From the forwarder's perspective, he/she is happy that the receiver is happy. The relationship between them will also grow stronger.

## The second effect of Feedforward is to turn the forwarder's attention to his/her future as well

The second effect of Feedforward is that the forwarder's consciousness also turns into the future. You may think you are only feedforwarding to the receiver, but the effect bounces back to the forwarders too. The brain has an interesting function. It doesn't seem to make a clear distinction as to whether the uttered words are "for other people" or "for myself." This gives rise to an intrinsic reinforcement mechanism resulting in a "virtuous cycle" that quickly gains in strength.

**Figure 13: The mechanism of Feedforward**

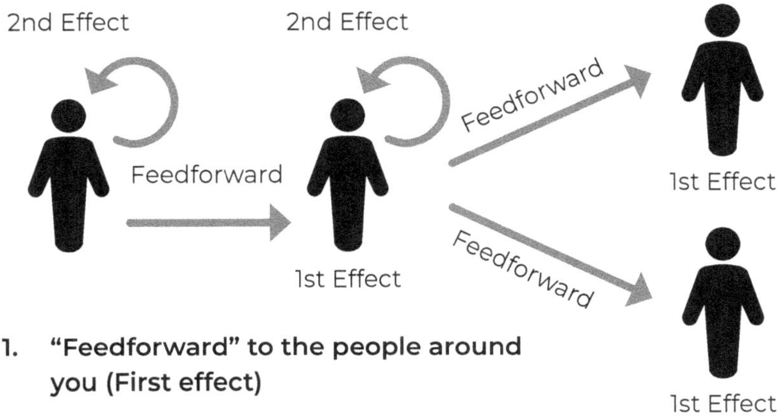

1. **"Feedforward" to the people around you (First effect)**

2. **The "Feedforward" will come back to yourself (Second effect)**

Source: KAZUYOSHI HISANO AND CONOWAY, INC.

It's often said, "Don't say bad things about others." Why? Given the characteristics of the brain, the reason is obvious. This is because the brain perceives it as if you were speaking ill of yourself. The words you intended to say to others will bounce back to you.

At lunchtime, someone may ask you, "Don't you want to eat ramen[35]?" Those who asked this question may have intended to ask others, but unconsciously, they are saying what they want themselves.

Forwarders ask receivers, "What do you want to do from now on?" This is nothing different from asking the question to yourself, given the nature of the brain. Those who feedforward to others many times are also feedforwarding

---

35 Ramen is Japanese noodles, very popular in Japan.

to themselves many times. As a result, the more feedforward you do to others, the happier you become.

I am the one who feedforwards most often in the world. So, I am also the one in the world most frequently asking myself the question "What do you want to do from now on? I am certain that it will continue to deepen my future-oriented thinking.

A proverb says, "Compassion is not for others." There are cases where it is wrongly interpreted, but the real meaning is, "It's not just for the sake of the other person that you should show compassion. Someday it will come back to you in return, so you should be kind to everyone." Feedforward is a method that faithfully practices: "Compassion is not for others."

## Examples of organizations where Feedforward has become the norm

What does an organization look like where *Feedforward* has become the norm? Let's expand on this bit. First, everyone is interested in others' dreams or goals and understands that each person is aiming for different things. At the same time, they are feeling happy to be working in the same organization. Here's what people say about each other:

"I don't understand why he likes football, but I do like him as a person. He talks about football very passionately. I think being passionate about something is good. I think he is doing his job very well. Although I am not as passionate about football as he is, I wouldn't mind joining him if he asks me out to see a game on the weekends." This is how they see each other. They sincerely want the happiness and success of others.

With such a team, business results will naturally improve. Their communication is good, and teamwork is outstanding. Their productivity is high, and they demonstrate persistence in difficult situations. It's the strength of an organization that is *doing what they want to do.*

Let's take one company, for example; their existing business is growing at 140% per year, and new businesses are being launched one after another. The number of employees has increased, and the turnover rate has decreased. The lending from banks is favorable, and a positive cycle is established. Employees say, "We're so busy," and "It's really hard," but all seem to be happy. Everything is just great.

So, are there any traps that organizations where *Feedforward* has become the norm are prone to fall into? I would point out that the rate of growth can be so fast that management's ability may not keep up with the change. As a countermeasure, management should continue to study and engage with others in the business who have been managing their companies at a similar rate of growth.

It may seem too fast at first, but once it is normalized, it will eventually settle down. When you drove at 40 mph for the first time at the driving school, you might have felt the speed was fast, but once you get your driver's license and start driving on public roads, you will forget that feeling. The same is true for management's sense of speed.

There is one more trap. Again, growth can be so fast that it may cause a gap between employees and their families. Therefore, we need to have a system to involve the family in the growth phase. Periodically you should organize family events, such as office tours or barbecues to help the families understand how the company is and where it's heading. Leaving your family behind in these phases can be a cause for creating a dream killer (to be discussed later). You need to be careful.

One more thing to confirm. What should we do if someone who acts completely based on the past has a position of power in the company? The benefit of *Feedforward* is that you can feedforward to any receiver. Your receiver can be the CEO or anyone. Having said that, there are stubborn people in every company. So, first, let's feedforward those whom you can most likely influence. If those around you gradually develop a more forward-looking mindset, it becomes harder for anyone to continue to be anchored in the past.

There is something that I would like you to be mindful of. Don't think, "I will change people with *Feedforward*." That is not necessary. *Feedforward* is not a method to change people. It is to make every moment better in a small way. If the *Feedforward* conversation leads the receiver to experience future-oriented thinking for even five minutes, you should feel good about it.

For example, let's say you are on the train with your boss. You are listening to his lecture, nodding and saying "Yes,

I see. That's right." And then you ask him "By the way, what's next for that project?" Let him talk about the future. This is also *Feedforward*. Your boss will change maybe for just five minutes. When you get off the train and return to the office, he will get back to being his old self. But it's OK because you were able to invite him into the future for five minutes.

You don't have to transform all at once. As you accumulate these changes, you will gradually spend more time leaning toward the future and enjoy the process.

## Interviews using future-oriented thinking

What would happen if you were to interview your subordinates with future-oriented thinking? First, the subordinate's face will light up. Of course, it will. They might be prepared for criticism about their performance, but instead, they are allowed to talk about their future. Your subordinates will become more confident in themselves with this approach.

However, if you try to let them have *future-oriented thinking* suddenly, you may not be able to continue the conversation well. If you ask them "What would you like to do?" you may only get answers such as "Well, there is nothing in particular that I want to do," or "I want to complete this job and go out for a drink." There is no need to be discouraged with such responses. It's just that your subordinate is not used to future-oriented thinking. In such cases, it is okay to just spend time on small talk. There is no need to prolong the process. Keep the conversation casual and try to see if there's a chance to touch upon the future.

"Where do you live?" "I live in Chicago." "Since when?" "It's been about ten years now." So far it has been completely past-oriented thinking. This is where you say, "Will you continue to live there going forward?" – slipping into the question of future-oriented thinking. "Well, I'd like to live somewhere closer to the office, but my kid is already in school." "Yes sure, I see." It may be only 30 seconds or so, but you had a conversation of future-oriented thinking. You can make a few such attempts on an ad-hoc basis. It can even be 10 seconds or 20 seconds. It will be effective.

Certain phrases should not be used in the interview with future-oriented thinking. You should avoid asking questions that direct them consciously or unconsciously into the past; for example, "Why did you do that?" or "What made you think that?" or "What got you started on that?"

As mentioned above, when *Feedforward* does not work, it can't be helped that conversation is switched to mundane talk and becomes past-oriented. However, when the interaction becomes based on future-oriented thinking, don't bring up the phrases that are better avoided. This is because the receiver's consciousness jumps to the past and he/she will remember the situation at that time. This is a waste of time.

Any communication that helps the other person to look into the future is *Feedforward*. Even if it's only for a short time. Try to find ways to guide the receiver's consciousness into the future.

## Performance appraisal with Feedforward

Many companies conduct performance appraisal interviews. During the interviews, employees' progress is evaluated against the goals they have set, and their supervisors provide advice and guidance. In this way, challenges toward subsequent goals are visualized. However, these traditional interviews are a product of past-oriented thinking.

So, what would *Feedforward*-based performance appraisal interviews look like? It's just that the order of conversation will be changed. It's fine to talk about the past as far as the evaluation itself is concerned. But, first, ask "What do you want to do from now on?"

You may start the conversation in this way, "Thank you for your time today. Well, let's get started. This is the annual performance appraisal interview. The first thing I would like you to talk about is what you want to do from now on. How do you want to move forward with your work? What are you aiming for? I think it would be easier to proceed with the interview if you could talk about these things. What do you think?"

The employee may get puzzled, wondering "As the performance appraisal is the subject for today, aren't we going to talk about what happened so far?" But still, the interviewee will answer what was asked. "Well, right now, I'm in charge of the XX branch, but it's in a stagnant situation. I'd like to grow it more and bring it up to a higher level. To do that, I need to learn more leadership. I have a child now, so I don't have much time to spare, but I want to make it somehow." At this moment, the receiver's consciousness is jumping into the future.

When the employee tries to talk about "what I want to do from now on," in the process of explaining it, he/she may naturally mention "what has happened so far." In this case, a starting point lies in the future, so the receiver won't be overly pulled toward the past. Of course, there are times when receivers don't talk about their past. That is no problem as well.

In a traditional performance appraisal interview, the boss tends to start by saying "This is how you have been doing until now." Then the interviewee will feel discouraged because they discuss the issues while still being pulled into the past. Afterward, when the boss says, "Now shall we talk about the future?" the interviewee will hardly hear it.

In the *Feedforward*-based performance appraisal interview, we talk in the order of *future→past→future* and close. Talking about the future twice and the past once and will be a sufficiently future-oriented discussion. It is the opposite of the traditional style of interview.

Of course, there's nothing wrong with talking about performance in depth. It should be done properly. However, it would be a waste of opportunity if your subordinate gets discouraged by the conversation.

There is a game called "Menko" in Japan. Players place palm-sized cards on the ground and keep some cards in hand. To win the game, you slap your card to flip over the opponent's cards on the ground and collect as many as possible.

However, you don't need to play so aggressively with *Feedforward*. Even if you can't flip a receiver's mind, all you need to do is let it slightly "float," which means guiding it toward the direction of the future.

With *Feedforward*, a ripple occurs in the receiver's mind. His/her mind is starting to look ahead. Whether the reaction is slow, or you can't see it from your side, a change is happening deep down inside his/her mind. So, there is nothing to worry about.

## Feedforward meeting and brainstorming

You must have heard of brainstorming. It is a meeting method where multiple participants share their opinions aiming to generate innovative and original ideas. The rules are set for the success of brainstorming, such as "Don't judge ideas," "Welcome unique ideas," "Value quantity over quality," and "Combine ideas." In brainstorming, you are allowed to say anything you want. It's okay to put out an analytical comment based on the past.

*Feedforward* can also be used to increase the effectiveness of brainstorming. I call it a *Feedforward Meeting*. It's a "brainstorming for the future," so to speak. Participants will list the "things they can" and "things they want to do in the future."

You don't have to turn all the meetings in your company into *Feedforward Meetings*. When you are conducting a regular meeting or a brainstorming, the chairperson or facilitator can say, "Let's switch over to *Feedforward* from now" if they feel the need for future-oriented thinking. The next part of the meeting is then devoted to future building discussions.

Figure 14: Increase the "level of futurism", "levels of abstraction" and "the distance from the comfort zone" of the ideas.

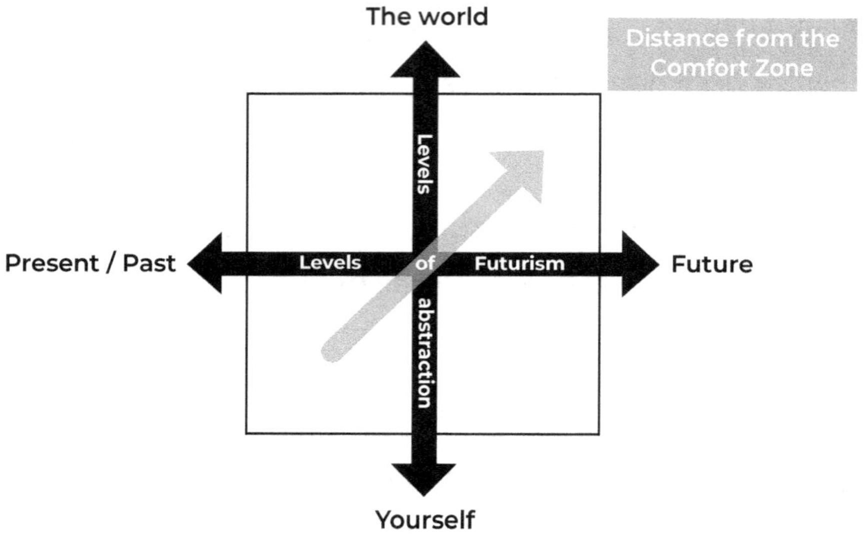


Source: KAZUYOSHI HISANO AND CONOWAY, INC.

The rules will be similar to those for the usual brainstorming. Let's take a look at the principles of *Feedforward Meeting*. "Don't judge ideas" and "On the ideas and comments that are generated, enhance the levels of futurism, levels of abstraction, and degree of distance from the comfort zone." These two are the rules.

The most important one is "Don't judge ideas." Don't deny any opinion. As the meeting proceeds the participants are conscious of enhancing *the levels of futurism, levels of abstraction*, and *degree of distance from the comfort zone*. (See Figure 14.)

During the discussions, it is important to confirm whether it is something "you really want to do." If the participants generate ideas with the thought that "the point is to say something big," they will end up just talking big, without achieving anything. It is fine to enlarge the scale of the ideas, but make sure to confirm if it is really *what we want to do*.

For your reference, I include the chart in Figure 15 which shows where people of various attributes look at from the two axes of "future and present/past" and "world and myself." In my CEO coaching, I encourage my clients to focus on the upper right quadrant for their activities to help them accelerate the speed to achieve success.

## Figure 15: Which quadrant are you looking at?

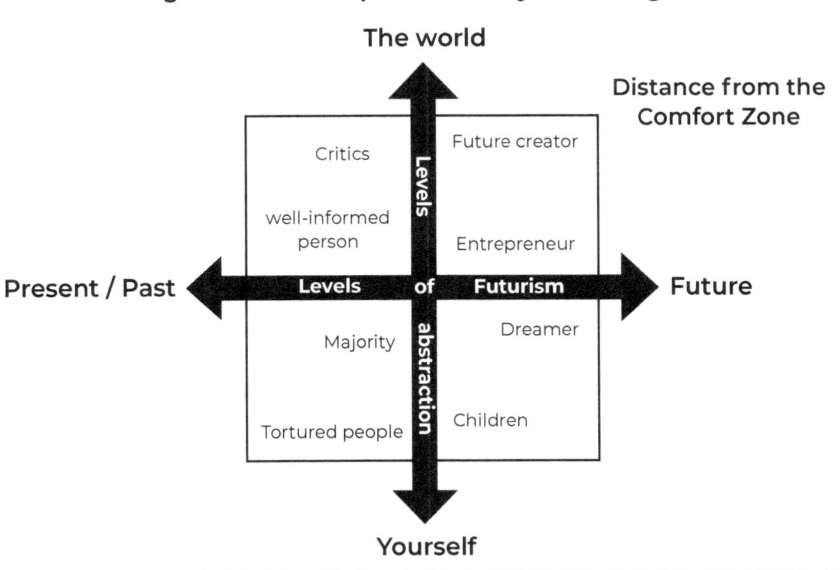


Source: KAZUYOSHI HISANO AND CONOWAY, INC.

## Can we Feedforward to family and friends?

*Feedforward* can be done to anyone including family and friends. As I already explained, it's easy to do this to your superiors as well. This contrasts with the difficulty of doing regular coaching for a boss or senior colleagues.

Ideally, you should feedforward in your daily conversations. Try to make any conversation *Feedforward* whenever you talk to others. Then, when it comes to a proper meeting, you can do it smoothly. *Feedforward* is not something that you "prepare well and do." Rather, you can achieve a better effect when it is spontaneous.

Even in conversations with people you haven't seen for a long time, you can ask them about their prospects with *Feedforward*. In many cases, however, we tend to ask them about the current state. Of course, we ask such questions because we are interested, but if we do so, we tie them to the past. It's a negative thing for them too. Putting our interests and concerns aside for the moment, focus the exchange on future-oriented thinking. That's what I usually do.

In my work, it's not uncommon for me to work with a client for months without knowing his/her background. Since our usual conversations are in *Feedforward* mode, I don't ask anything about his/her past. As a result, my client doesn't have a chance to talk about the past.

As for me, although the feeling of uncertainty continues for a while, I am used to it now. It's my job to lead clients to success without delving into their profiles. I find out later what he/she has done. As my clients don't get coaching just to talk about their life stories or small talk, my style is something very natural.

## Does focusing on the future lead to "neglect of the problem"?

*Feedforward* is done based on future-oriented thinking, but some people question this, wondering "It's good to look to the future, but is it okay to turn away from the status quo?", or "Isn't this just 'leaving the problem alone?" Let me answer. It is not a problem at all. Rather, if you start by looking at the current problem, it will be harder to come up with good solutions.

Conversely, when you think ahead to the future on what you are aiming for by *Feedforward*, your brain starts to look for what you need to do to make that future a reality.

When you are facing a problem, you are bound to think about "Why it happened?" However, before doing so, it is better to first think about "what you want to do," "what you need to do," and "how you will do it," and then look at the current situation. This can make it surprisingly easy to solve the problem.

Let's say you're having breakfast, and you spill some coffee on your clothes. You are in a hurry as you have an appointment with an important person. At such times, you tend to try to do something about the stain. This too should not be so difficult if you deal with it through future-oriented thinking. All you must do is to change the clothes right away. Take the stained clothes to a dry cleaner later. There is no problem with this.

Turning away from the status quo does not lead directly to neglect of the problem. Rather, looking to the future can hasten the resolution.

## Management people who are frustrated with their employees need future-oriented thinking

Always being frustrated and in a bad mood, there must be such people around you. This is not uncommon among managers as well. Management is in a position where it is acceptable to be blatantly frustrated. They are different from employees in that respect. But I recommend *Feedforward* to such people in top management positions. Look at the future of your company, the future of your employees, and your future. Then you can see what you need to do, and you will realize that there's more to do than get frustrated. There is no time to get frustrated, if you keep your eyes on the direction you want to go.

Why do managers get so frustrated? When we think about the reason for this, we come to the issue of *expectations*. They get frustrated because they have expectations. When their expectations of the company and employees are too high or misplaced, managers get frustrated. However, this miscalculation is due to poor judgment by the manager. Being frustrated itself is dysfunctional and meaningless. Even if it's unavoidable to be frustrated, one shouldn't take it out on other people. So long as the abilities of other people are accurately estimated, managers need not be frustrated anymore.

## Life is a series of failures, which is why future-oriented thinking works

Tadao Ando, one of Japan's leading architects, has written a book titled *Successive Defeats*. Mr. Ando has been competing in design competitions all over the world. As a result, he suffered more defeats than you would imagine from his glamorous career. The book *Successive Defeats* comes from a lecture given at the University of Tokyo Graduate School, about what he learned and thought from such experiences.

Hiroshi Aramata, a natural historian, said, "Life is like a chess game without a rook and bishop. It's only natural to be defeated." There is so much to learn from the attitudes of the two men.

I can say there are many times in life when we experience defeat. To me, "the summer is hot" and "people are repeatedly defeated" don't sound much different. Losing is never something to be ashamed of. If you don't give up, you are always *halfway through the game* and never a *loser*.

"I have not failed. I've just found 10,000 ways that won't work." These words were spoken by Thomas Edison, the master of invention.

There is no way you can win every battle in life. Those who try a lot and lose a lot will thrive; you won't even feel like you lost. A successful person has nothing but future-oriented thinking.

**CHAPTER 6**

# The Power to Know Yourself: Cause

---

"Cause has two major attributes:
strength and altitude"

*Cause Theory* is the third essential of the
*Gold Vision Method*[36]. This is very important.

*Cause*[37] is an English word meaning *source* or *root*.
You can rephrase it as *purpose* or *motive*.

---

36  Gold Vision, Feedforward and Cause

37  Cause is something without which something else would not happen. Cause is also reason for doing or feeling something.

Every person has a *Cause* that they inherently believe in. The strength and altitude of the cause determine the degree of happiness and success of the person. Looking from another angle, *Cause* is also a fundamental understanding of what you value and consider important and why you want to set that goal.

*Cause* solely belongs to the individual. Only you need to recognize it for yourself; it is not something that should be imposed on others or by others. Similar terms to cause include formative experiences, values, and cherished matters.

Now, *Cause* can be measured on two scales: *strength* and *altitude*. I call the two together the size of *Cause*.

*Strength* is the degree of how much you believe in that *Cause*.

*Altitude* refers to the degree to which a *Cause* is accepted by others with universality and public benefit. It could be rephrased as *altruism*.

The cause is formed based on past experiences. Our behavior is guided by our cause or purpose. Basically, it is very difficult to change the cause itself or change the strength or altitude of the cause using our will.

How then can we cultivate a *Cause* with strength and altitude? Let's look at it from one example.

Mr. A is a CEO who wants to get his business off the ground. There are two reasons why he wants to get his business off the ground: "I want to make a lot of money and make my family happy," and "I want to show the world what I can do." The reason why he wants to "make a lot of money" and "show his power" is because he believes that "a lot of money is necessary to be happy," "being capable is valuable," and "it is important to be recognized by the world."

Here, Mr. A's assumptions are these three; "A lot of money is necessary to be happy," "Being competent is valuable," and "Being recognized by the world is important."

Now, let us think about the strength and altitude of Mr. A's cause. How strongly he believes in the three causes is his strength. Mr. A strongly believes that "a lot of money is necessary to be happy" and at the same time, he strongly believes that "being competent is valuable" and that "he wants the world to recognize his competence." If he is successful in his business, he can fulfill all these things at the same time and that's why he is working so hard. Therefore, the strength of Mr. A's cause is quite high.

What about the altitude of the cause? There seem to be a lot of people who think "I need money," "Being competent is valuable," or "Being recognized by the world is important," so the universality seems to be high.

On the other hand, public benefit is not so high. Even if Mr. A thinks that "A lot of money is necessary to be happy," or that "Being competent is important," or that "Being recognized by the world is important," it doesn't help other people that much.

To explain this from another perspective, *Cause* is, so to speak, a conviction for a certain person that "It's just the way it is." To the question "What makes you think that?", the only possible answer would be "Because I think that way," and cannot be drilled down any further.

Figure 16: How to check the strength and altitude of your Cause

| The thing that you are putting effort on | The reason that is important | Cause (Belief) |
|---|---|---|
| why → | why → | |
| Get the business off the ground | • I want to earn a lot of money and make my family happy<br>• I want to show that I am a capable person | • We need a lot of money to be happy<br>• Being competent is worth while<br>• Being recognized by the world is important |

You can check the strength and altitude of the Cause

Source: KAZUYOSHI HISANO AND CONOWAY, INC.

For example, "Rakkyo (Japanese leek) goes well with curry and rice" or "Soy sauce must be poured on eggs sunny-side up" may also become a type of *Cause*. In the latter case, the altitude is not so high, but if the strength is very high, there is a possibility of research and development of a special soy sauce for eggs sunny-side up and making it a hit.

Evaluating the cause by strength and altitude allows us to measure the social impact of the cause. More to the point, the impact is strengthened when the *Cause* is tied to your goal.

## Cause is generated by experience

*Cause* is formed from your own experiences. It's an experience, so of course it is something that happened in the past. Causes are created through all the experiences, successes and setbacks in our lives, joys and sorrows, the social environment we have placed ourselves in, the communities we have belonged to, and the teachings we have received from our parents, teachers, and other influences.

Now, the goal is defined by the size of *Cause*, so the higher strength and altitude *Cause* has, the bigger the goal will be. When the goal is big, people are more likely to act on it. If *Cause* is not that big, a commensurate goal will be set. If the goal doesn't originate from your own cause, even if you try to technically set a larger goal, the goal you set once will become smaller to match your cause.

So, do we have to continue to live under a determined *Cause*? No, this is not the case. As mentioned above, *Cause* is based on the past. So long as we are alive, we are constantly creating a "new past" experience in the flow of time from the future to the present to the past. What happened an hour ago is the future from yesterday's viewpoint, but from the present, it is the past. The past just keeps increasing.

How we create this *new past* can have an impact on *Cause*. In other words, we can make a change to *Cause* using future-oriented thinking. Specifically, the bigger the goal becomes, the more *Cause* will be expanded.

Let's take an example. Suppose a person sees poor people while on a trip and thinks, "Poverty must be eradicated."

This is a *Cause* that comes from his own experience. However, the family he grew up in was not so poor. The cause is not that big. However, he continues to have a goal of eradicating poverty and spends his time getting involved in various activities. By doing so, he can make an impact on the cause. While he has not experienced poverty himself, it is still possible to expand *Cause* with involvement and time.

**Figure 17: The relationship between "Cause" and "Goal"**

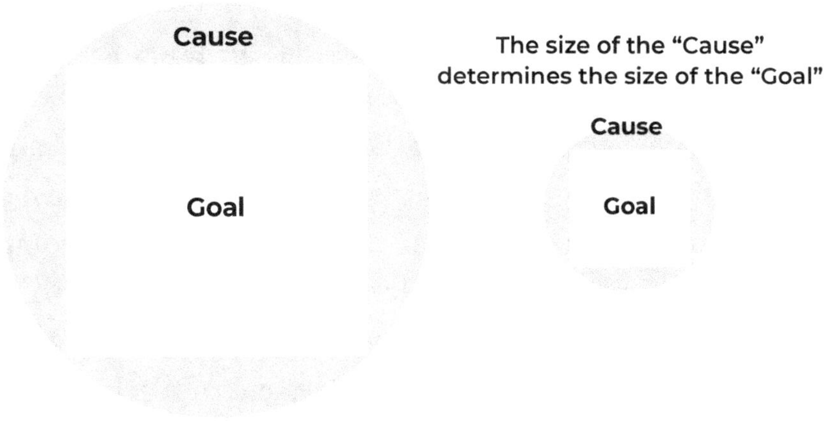

Cause

Goal

The size of the "Cause" determines the size of the "Goal"

Cause

Goal

- The size of the "Cause" ("strength" and "altitude") is represented by the size of the circle.
- The size of the "Goal" is represented by the size of the square.

Source: KAZUYOSHI HISANO AND CONOWAY, INC.

By going to the site, and listening to peoples' stories, he can increase his past experiences. He can do this because he has set the lofty goal of eradicating poverty. Without a goal, however much he experiences poverty, it wouldn't influence the cause at all.

Finding your *Cause* itself can take time. It could take five or ten years. There is no need to rush. Let's do it step-by-step. In the sense that our personal experience generates *Cause*, the proverb "Like father, like son" can be fairly accurate. If the father is a member of parliament, the child is likely to be too. There are so many such examples. The way to turn this "Like father, like son" upside down is *Gold Vision* and *Feedforward*.

As for myself, I was good at teaching people, but I didn't think I would become a schoolteacher. As I thought about it many times, I felt that "teaching may be good for me," but at the time I wanted to do something else. I was unable to take the next step. However, before I knew it, I was gradually getting closer and closer to a teaching job. When I worked in a company, I had subordinates, things were going well because I was good at teaching.

Eventually, I came to realize my formative experience for coaching was when a classmate asked me to teach him to study at the age of seven. I taught him and he said, "I got it" at that point, but just before returning home, he said, "But I don't think I can do it." His parents were the kind of people who scolded their child saying, "There's no point in studying." I continued to teach him to study until the ninth grade. However, every time when we finished studying, he said "I cannot do this, can I?" I was tormented with a sense of helplessness. I kept saying to him every time, "Of course you can." These experiences have shaped my cause and led me to the present day over several decades.

## Do not be stuck in the past

There is a cardinal rule for the *Cause Theory*. That is, "think about your *Cause* only after you sufficiently acquire futuristic thinking." If you do it in the wrong order, you will only get the opposite effect.

Your cause is built on the foundation of your past experiences. More to the point, when you think about the cause, you tend to fall into backward thinking. You need to be careful about this. Past experiences and memories are related to each other. When you start thinking about your cause, you will start to notice many other things and may be caught up in the past. When you are immersed in the past, your ability to move forward into the future is greatly diminished. You should avoid that.

Don't think about *Cause* until you've fully mastered futuristic thinking. It's safer that way.

I've been coming up with the concept of a person's *Cause* since I was in my twenties. As I tried to move into the future, the question "Who am I?" popped into my head many times. After much deliberation, I concluded that a deep understanding of myself would be a driving force. However, at the same time, I also understood, "If I don't have a firm vision of the future, the driving force won't be strong." So, I usually talk about *Cause* only after I've completed my explanation of *Gold Vision* and *Feedforward*.

# Five elements which determine the level of authenticity

I have already briefly explained the "levels of authenticity." It's a trait that people who achieve outstanding results possess. You could say it's a pre-condition for *genius*. A person with a high level of authenticity possesses the following five elements at a high level:

1. A high degree of distance from the status quo: Always set goals *outside of the status quo*. (Think big.)
2. A high level of futurism: Always look into the *future*. (Look far ahead.)
3. A high level of abstraction: Always look at the world from a higher level. (Think creatively and observe patterns rather than details.)
4. A high strength of Cause: Strongly believe in your Cause. (This enables you to get others involved and gain support from others.)
5. A high altitude of Cause: Have a Cause with a high degree of public interest. (This also helps you to get others involved and gain support from them.)

Why these five? There is a correlation between the "degree of distance from the status quo," "levels of futurism," and "levels of abstraction." The higher the "levels of futurism" and "level of abstraction," the higher the degree of "distance from the status quo" will naturally become. The reverse is also true. This relationship is supported by the "strength of the cause" and the "altitude of the cause." The five elements are interconnected.

Let me elaborate a little more on the *altitude* of Cause and the *strength* of Cause. Many people have a vague sense of wanting to eliminate war from the world. This is a Cause with high altitude. However, if the person in question does not feel strongly about it, the strength will be low. This won't make anything happen. Conversely, even with a low altitude, if you do strongly believe in yourself, you have a good chance of succeeding.

For business expansion, strength is more important than the altitude of the Cause. For example, let's say someone wants to paint a plastic model in color, but is not satisfied with the existing paint. Eventually, he decides that "it must be this color" and makes it by himself. The cause does not have a high altitude, but it's an example of high strength. Although it may not be of interest to most people, it is strongly supported by some enthusiasts. Strength is directly related to passion.

If such a passionate person eventually raises the levels of abstraction and the degree of distance from the status quo, he/she makes special colors available in other situations or changes the concept of paint itself drastically; it is possible to achieve results of a different dimension.

## Management with high altitude can move on to the next stage

While the strength of Cause leads to passion and the creation of unique businesses, the higher the "altitude of Cause" of the management, the greater the likelihood that the business will grow. Management with a high "altitude of Cause" has an overwhelming advantage over those who don't because they have the following characteristics:

- Can recruit talented people and are supported by internal and external supporters.
- Are loved by customers.
- Can get the support from society in general.

It was in November 2010 that the International Organization for Standardization (ISO) formulated the international standard "ISO 26000" under the name of "social responsibility".

It is good if the management really cares about the "public interest," but it is not a good idea to just jump on this bandwagon without conviction.

To take one example, Masayoshi Son, the founder of the SoftBank Group, appears to be seriously aiming to promote an information revolution. If you set a solid direction for the public interest, you should be able to move forward with your business despite the risks.

## Keep your efficacy high and prevent your goals from becoming small

"Efficacy works as a tension pole for the goal." I'll explain a bit more here, including its relevance to Cause. The cause determines the size of the goal, and at the same time, as the goal becomes bigger Cause is also impacted.

Even if you dare to set a large goal, the size of the Cause is fixed, so if you leave it alone, the goal will shrink to fit the Cause. The way to keep the goal big is to use efficacy as a "tension pole" to pull you up.

Efficacy is the degree to which you feel "I can do it." The higher this is, the easier it is to maintain a high goal. Eventually, it starts to impact Cause, and changes will occur. Having said that, there will be times when your heart is about to be broken. Are there any tips for keeping your efficacy high?

Essentially, it's hard to keep your efficacy high on your own. It's important to put yourself amid people with high efficacy and interact with them. It is necessary to make efforts (devise ways) to create such an environment.

As you can already see, *the power to see the future* (goal setting) and *the power to believe in yourself* (efficacy) are in one set. Furthermore, please understand that they are inextricably linked to Cause.

Figure 18: The relationship between "Cause" and "Goal", and "Efficacy"

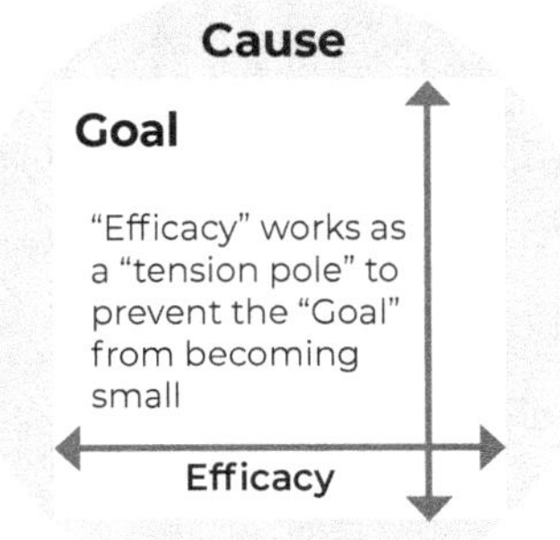


Source: KAZUYOSHI HISANO AND CONOWAY, INC.

## Profit is a sign of gratitude

Let's confirm one premise. Making money in and of itself is not a bad thing at all. It is a good thing. When I talk about Cause, some people seem to take it as if I'm arguing that making money is evil. I want to emphasize that it is a misunderstanding. It's quite simple; those who have a large Cause are also more likely to make big money. Why? To make a lot of money, you need to please a lot of people deeply. For this, it is advantageous to have a larger Cause.

So, can't people with small Causes make money? As I mentioned earlier, for the time being, we have no choice but to deal with the current Cause. Keep your goals high and try to expand the Cause. By doing so, you will become a person who can deeply please people, and your earning power will gradually increase.

It's also important to grow your Cause from the perspective that profit is a sign of gratitude from your customers.

## Understanding subconscious motivation

"The past is always new, and the future is always nostalgic" – this is the title of a book by photographer Daido Moriyama. This sensation is similar to the feeling when we encounter our own *Cause*. I've always wanted to reach these grounds, but it's not easy.

Encountering your *Cause* is also about getting to know yourself. To *know yourself* means to meet both your past and your future self. Knowing who you have been in the past, what you could be like in the future, and understanding what you need to do to get there. If you can do this, you will be at peace. You will feel mild elation. In the brain, dopamine will be secreted.

This state of being suffused in euphoria lasts 24 hours a day, 365 days a year. This is what is required of management of *one-to-100*. As for employees, 24 hours a day may be difficult, but if they are in the state for more of those hours, the entire company will gain the power to drive forward calmly and steadily. We sometimes see business books that tell us to create a frenzied state, but it would be hard to achieve *one-to-100* that way. Above all, it doesn't last.

Let me change the expression. *Cause* is the answer to "Why am I doing this now?" To know your *Cause* is to know yourself. The *self,* in this case, may be described as *subconscious.* The future and the past are contained in this subconscious. "Why I have done this" is not very important. The main points are "what I am trying to do from now" and "why I am doing this now."

When you have a clear idea of your *Cause* and are convinced of it, your work and your days become simple. It will make you feel refreshed. It will also make your brain work more clearly.

This is difficult to explain to those who have never experienced it before, but those who have experienced it at least once should be able to understand this immediately.

Once your goal and personal *Cause* are clarified, there will be no more doubt. I hope that as many people as possible will have this kind of experience.

**CHAPTER 7**

# The Power to Execute: Execution

"If you don't take action, nothing will happen"

In this chapter, I will discuss the *power to execute*. If you don't take action in the first place, nothing will happen. However, there is a mechanism in the human brain that makes us feel as if we achieved something just by thinking about it. This feature is a two-edged sword, so you need to be careful with your balance and make good use of it.

The *Gold Vision Method* is a cognitive science-based methodology that makes you want to act naturally. So, by nature, there is no such thing as the mindset of "I have to take action." However, the power of the *comfort zone* is stronger than you may imagine.

At the same time, there is also the problem of the *dream killer*. It can be thought of as a being that stands in the way of someone's dream to come true. The biggest dream killer would be yourself. With the strength of the comfort zone, coupled with the presence of the dream killer, there are a few people and organizations that can take action.

When the sense of reality of the world of the goal is heightened, achieving it becomes the norm, and that state of being becomes the new comfort zone. Then, you feel a strong sense of discomfort with the fact that the comfort zone is not the reality yet, and you naturally want to act on it.

However, it is a bit delicate to maintain the right balance between the imagined future and the required action. The sense of reality must be heightened so much that you have the feeling that it has been realized, but if you have a delusion or illusion, you won't do anything. This balance is subtle and difficult.

I recommend you get involved with people who are realizing the world of their goals. You should feel that "I'm still lacking," or that "I haven't been able to do this yet." It's the confirmation you need to act.

To achieve *one-to-100*, you need the *power to execute*. Putting it the other way around, you can achieve *one-to-100* if you can get the mighty *power to execute*.

## Power to plan "planning"

If you think about it in terms of the *Feedforward* concept, the power to plan may not feel right. Some of you may think of the PDCA cycle. The power to plan here is something a little different. It's the backward calculation that your brain does automatically after you set a goal.

Once the goal is determined, you can vaguely see the steps depending on your knowledge and experience in the field. The more knowledge and experience you have, the clearer and more detailed steps will be seen. The power to plan is to verbalize and embody these steps. We highly recommend this.

The important thing to note is that you shouldn't make the plan with a pre-conceived idea with the thought, such as "I do this because it was like this with my past experiences."

When it comes to starting a new business or launching a new product, this kind of pre-conceived idea is often used. It's a process where you collect data and develop a plan. At first glance, it looks good, but this is an optimization of the past. At best, it's just an optimization of the current situation. It is not certain if these plans will work tomorrow.

The measures that will work tomorrow will have a better chance to work if they are considered from the future's perspective. Moreover, the goal is not something that we can achieve without a clear aim. It's the future we eagerly wait for. Be careful not to get caught up in your past experiences when working backward from the future and embodying the steps you see.

1. Distant goals naturally determine the plan.
   Just let your brain work. Make yourself relax.

2. You need a plan to get help from those around you.
   With *Gold Vision,* it is believed that "being able to plan is the same as being able to execute." In Gold Vision goals are something that you visualize, as if they have already been realized. If you can see it, you should be able to execute it.

   However, the reality is that there are many things that one person cannot do alone. So, we show our plan to others and seek their support. The skill of writing up a plan is one of the essential elements of mobilizing people and getting them involved. It could easily be overlooked, but it is very important.

3. The PDCA cycle is not bad across the board.
   It is good to start with planning (P) after setting a big goal. Don't forget that setting a goal is always a prerequisite.

4. Writing it out will get your brain moving.
   It's hard to move forward if you only think about it in your head. Let's take a step to write it out on paper or typing it into your computer or mobile device. You can look at it objectively and naturally want to move forward.

## The power to overcome difficulties "overleap"

The reality of management is truly a series of difficulties. The shortcut to becoming a management of *one-to-100* is to learn how to overcome the obstacles. You could say it's the most fundamental thing. The power to overcome difficulties is related to *the levels of abstraction.* Most difficulties can be solved by raising your perspective and making it feel less daunting. If you can get two levels up, it even looks like an opportunity.

## 1. The self-image that "I can overcome this" is the driving force.

It can be a fun experience if you know that you can overcome any difficulty. It can even be quite exciting. It's like the fun and excitement of a game that you know *you can win.* As soon as you think, "I can't get over it," you will be in a lot of pain.

There is no such thing as *insurmountable difficulties* in this world. All difficulties are meant to be enjoyed by nature. Truly successful people seem to enjoy a challenge. What is also important here is *the power to believe in yourself* (efficacy). *Efficacy* is something that doesn't require evaluation by others. It doesn't matter how strongly other people think it is impossible, so long as you believe "I can do it."

## 2. Make full use of past experience.

Let your past achievements turn into a source of efficacy in the future. The important thing is what you can do from now on. Let's take promotions and appraisals in a company. These decisions are generally made based on past performance. Instead of this why don't you make your judgments based on *the power to overcome difficulties in the future*? There will be much fewer cases as in "this is not what I had expected" after a promotion or appraisal.

Incidentally, regarding job titles and promotions, it is half-jokingly said in the American business world "All executives are incompetent." This means everyone successful will be promoted continuously until a point they cannot go up anymore, and the promotions stop. The result is that all roles are occupied by people who have reached their level of incompetence and, therefore, cannot succeed in their jobs.[38]

So, how do we measure the power for the future? This is a very difficult problem to solve. The conclusion is to judge the employee by *the levels of abstraction* in his/her approach to problems.

## 3. "Disastrous Experience" is the deciding factor.

Job skills are forged in the field. I have always felt that way. There are a lot of things going on in the field that could be called a "dreadful scene." By experiencing and overcoming them, your power will grow. Maintain a high level of abstraction while encountering a dreadful scene. This is what is at the core of the power to overcome difficulties. Only those

---

38 In fact, this is called "The Peter Principle" after Lawrence J Peter's business satire book published in 1969. Basically, someone's success in a smaller role does not tell anything about their success in a bigger role. – Editor

who can see the situation from a bird's eye view while being involved in it will be able to overcome the situation. The best way to develop people is to have them go through a tough situation.

Appropriate attention is also necessary for cases where the disastrous experience became traumatic. Trying to force yourself to try again after failing can be a *have-to* work.

If you were to apply the principles, you would leverage the visualization of "imagine what is working." However, even if you try to do this while remembering the *painful* and *bitter* feelings that you have gained through failure, you will inevitably end up with an attitude of *escape*. Actions taken while escaping will not produce good results. The turning point will be whether or not you can recognize that "I am apprehensive about this challenge because of what I experienced at that time." The key is whether you can recognize the trauma as a trauma.

## 4. Sharing "disastrous experiences."

If your employees are struggling during a rough patch, consider creating opportunities for them to hear from senior colleagues. Some companies encourage executives to share their disastrous experiences. However, we must be mindful to ensure that these talks do not turn into mere bragging. It's better to carry out these conversations seriously in a conference room setting.

## 5. How to create an "environment where you can fail."

There used to be a custom in Japan to "dare to drop a dear subordinate into a valley." It is a method of education based on the proverb, "The lion drops its child into a deep valley." It is said that a lion drops the newborn into a deep valley and raises only those with high vitality who come up. Taking it from there, it means to dare to challenge the person you truly care about so that he/she grows.

However, today, most young employees do not understand the meaning of "dare to drop into the valley." If you do it carelessly, it may become an obstacle to growth and could cause irreparable harm, not only to the subordinate but also to the manager.

Still, there is a need to develop talent. I focus on creating an environment in which *people can fail* in ways that are appropriate for today's society. It's not the small failures that truly develop the younger generation; rather, it is only when they face mid- to larger-scale failures that they can make significant progress.

The first thing to do is to let them take the plunge. Even though it may not be intended, the situation may occur where the employee realizes, "The result was not what I expected." After all, that's part of the job. It's best to have these experiences when one is still young. To facilitate this, the organization to which one belongs should foster a culture that supports failure.

No matter how much we encourage *challenges*, employees don't take the plunge. Only with a culture of encouraging *failure* can they become less hesitant to take on *challenges*. If you don't try, you won't ever fail. Does your company maintain an environment where you can fail?

## 6. What to do with those who can't get over it?

I can't stress enough the importance of encouraging young people to take on challenges. The future of an organization would be disastrous if people just sit in their positions instead of taking on challenges when they should have done so, and they are promoted to executive positions one after another. It is unfortunate that in this era of rapid change, a board of directors is dominated by people who can only *do a flawless job*. A little bit of mischievousness is just fine.

On the other hand, some people are unable to overcome difficulties. Responding to them is also an important point. The basics are quite simple. It's all about *waiting*. The only thing a boss can do is to believe that *he/she can do it eventually*.

However, the work comes with a deadline. If you don't think you can make it in time, you should explain it to him/her and let another person handle it.

If your organization has a culture that values challenge, you should consider up front, "What if he/she tried and it didn't work." To put it metaphorically, it's like a pitching change in a baseball. It can be frustrating for the pitcher to be substituted, but when considering the team, it may be unavoidable. For those who have to be replaced, the change does not mean a dead end. Of course, it's important to ensure they are given another opportunity."

## The power to continue steadily "steadiness"

I'm sure you're familiar with the parable of *The Tortoise and the Hare*. There is a lesson in this story. "No matter how capable you are, if you are arrogant and let your guard down, you will miss the opportunity. On the other hand, even if your ability is low, if you work steadily and with focus, you will get great results in the end."

This story is also valid in the business world. In the end, it's the *tortoise* that wins. Although blessed with talent, the overconfident *hare* wouldn't be a winner.

Even if you have a groundbreaking idea, if you can't execute it, it's just an idea. If you don't try to do it, at best, you are just a player who could have won but didn't. There are so many examples of such in the business world.

Here are a few key points that will help you develop your *power to continue steadily.*

## 1. The power to keep working toward a distant goal.

I already talked about the mechanism by which proper goal-setting can lead to success. If you fully understand how it works, you can *keep going*. On the other hand, if you lack understanding, you will not be able to decide when it is "time to quit" or "continue."

*The time to quit* is the moment when you lose interest. That moment doesn't come in the form of recognition that "I've lost interest." Rather, it's a form of "I had lost interest before I knew it."

## 2. If you stop, there's nothing left.

---

We move toward the goal that we sincerely desire. This is a normal and noble act. However, unfortunately, our society doesn't always respect that attitude. Aren't there people around you who are whispering to you, "It's time to grow up?" Every time I was told to "grow up," I shouted in my mind "I don't know what that means!"

In Japan today, "people who give up on their dreams" are called "adults." How many children want to become such adults?

Let me confirm again. You don't have to give up in the middle of the process. We don't have to follow such advice, or even listen to it. The "time to give up" is not something that is forced by others. It's something that you decide if you lose interest. It's very good to be persistent in what you want to do. Of course, it doesn't mean that you have to give up all the other roles you need to play. You can keep on doing what needs to be done. If you don't have time, then do what you can to the extent possible. "Lack of time" is not the reason that you cannot do it. It's better to have time than not, but time is not an absolute necessity.

You don't have to give up because you care about someone else's opinion or feelings. Remember the balance wheel. Do what you want to do and do it well.

## 3. Are "hares" and "grasshoppers" unhappy?

In fairy tales such as the one above *The Tortoise and the Hare* and *The Ant and the Grasshopper*[39], the hare and the grasshopper are positioned as if they were unhappy. However, I don't think they are necessarily unhappy.

It's because everything is a choice, and you are responsible for the consequences of your decisions. The key is "What goal did the hare or grasshopper have?" The outcome seen from the outside has nothing to do with the person's satisfaction. If they rested or played without knowing, "resting or playing here will result in losing the race or having trouble in winter," then they lacked knowledge or understanding. But if they knew about it and still took a break (played), they have made responsible decisions.

What goals the hares and grasshoppers were envisioning are rarely mentioned in the story. The hare's goal may not have been to win the race but to enjoy walking along the

---

39 In the story, the **grasshopper** illustrates the **theme** of "First be prepared, then find time to play." The **Ant** is the character who is preparing for the winter by storing up food while the **grasshopper** is playing around. The **grasshopper** says he doesn't need to worry with winter because he has enough food right now.

way. The grasshopper may have simply chosen to enjoy the pleasures of summer life rather than to survive in winter. That itself is their choice.

Again, it's the tortoise that wins the race in the end. However, I feel that it is somehow misleading to only convey the message of "be diligent" through the stories ignoring goal setting. It all depends on the goal. The hare and the grasshopper might have been satisfied with their lives. On the other hand, it may not be necessarily that the tortoise and the ant have lived a satisfying life.

## 4. Aligning yourself with the organization.

The key to alignment is the commonality in the goals of the organization and individuals. If you can find a common point or area in the organization's balance wheel, or in the individual's balance wheel, at a certain level of abstraction, it will work.

Individuals feel happy when they have achieved or are moving toward a goal that the organization and the individual can share. As a result, the organization will also be happy. They can feel happiness without being at odds with each other. That's the ideal situation.

There are some important assumptions to confirm. When an organization gets results, employees get promotions, their income rises, and their social status gets higher. It has been assumed that employees will be happier as a result.

That's why so much effort has been put in to improve the performance of the organization.

However, the situation has changed, especially since the beginning of the 21st century. It's because people started to realize that "happy organizations are the ones that grow." Rather than "having grown results in happiness," it is "being happy results in growth." When you think about this, you can see that it is imperative to help employees to achieve personal goals.

Of course, it will be a problem if your organization is not able to achieve its goals while individuals achieve their personal goals. The organization and the individual must find common goals that can be achieved at the same time. It's a state where continuing for yourself is benefiting the organization as well.

In the past, people restrained themselves and worked for the organization. But it's hard to do, and it does not fit with the times. We are moving into an era where organizations are respecting individuals' goals.

## 5. A corporate culture where determination is appreciated.

The culture of an organization is determined by "what kind of people are made into stars." I encourage people to "honor those who continue steadfastly on the path they decide." Then, the number of people who "keep going" will surely increase.

The important thing here is that the people being admired "set their own goals and move toward the goals while achieving good results." It's not enough to simply be obedient. It's not enough just to "do what is told" or "don't move unless you are told."

## 6. The need for unpredictability.

In Item 5, I mentioned the importance of respecting those who put steady efforts into carrying out what they decided to do. On the other hand, we also need those who are *capricious*[40] or impulsive, to complement the steadfast people. People with capriciousness, can excel and achieve good results in a short period. They have agility, but not much endurance. We need to persist with those capricious people as well. Just favoring those who stay with the company long is not a good strategy, as we may end up losing truly excellent talents. *Capricious* and *steadfast* are polarities. It is not an issue of which is better.

Let's value the balance here. Organizations are revitalized by fostering both *long-distance runners* and *sprinters*.

---

40  Capricious is "given to sudden and unaccountable changes of mood or behavior." – Dictionary

**CHAPTER 8**

# The Power to Mobilize the Organization: Autonomy[41]

"Life is about choices, and you have the ability to choose. You always have had this ability. I suggest that not only do you have the ability, you have the responsibility to make choices for yourself. It is your life, and you are in the driver's seat, if you choose to be."

~ LOU TICE

---

41 **Autonomy or self-motivation.** The organization needs to operate autonomously and in a decentralized manner. With people working from home, especially during the pandemic, it is important for them to possess the necessary skills to perform their jobs effectively.

## The group of people who makes up the comfort zone

So far, I have covered the foundation of the *one-to-100* concept. In Chapter 8, let me get to the core of it.

A comfort zone is not confined to an individual, but it forms around the people who come together. If you understand the nature of a comfort zone, you can greatly increase the power of your organization to achieve goals. When all the members of the organization are unified in pursuing something greater and visualizing the comfort zone of the future collectively, the power to attain it becomes overwhelmingly strong and people will have the sense of being enveloped by the future.

What if such power is generated spontaneously? For this purpose, too, it is essential that the goal is appropriately shared.

## Successful organizations function autonomously and spontaneously

You would all agree that the changes happening in the business environment continue to accelerate. Bureaucratic organizations will not survive, and agile competitors will move further and further ahead. A simple comparison of large corporations with new ventures may not necessarily apply here, but generally speaking, large corporations tend to be slower in decision-making.

Surely, the organizational approval mechanism is important. However, we should minimize such processes given the current business environment. The best way would be to revise your unnecessary approval practices as you detect them, while you are carrying out your business. Those companies that are already simplifying such decision-making and managing practices are indeed growing.

Well then, concretely speaking, what is the level of minimal necessity? The answer is in your intuitions that come to you by setting a goal. In other words, the intuition derived from the goal you have set will teach you. Since it is intuition, it differs from person to person. However, all members are united under a common goal. Thus, you can expect their intuitions to result in unison. If you feel certain rules are necessary to proceed smoothly, of course, you can set them in advance. It is essential to make these rules lean toward allowing autonomy and spontaneity. Otherwise, they can become a factor that drags the organization down. People who tend to argue and work against autonomy and spontaneity for various reasons may well be dream-killers. You need to take proper measures to deal with them.

Previously, I used a squad of criminal investigation detectives, as an example of the organization with autonomy and spontaneity. It is a kind of organization that carries out its work by sharing a common goal, holding high self-efficacy, believing in themselves that they can do it, and getting creative intuitions for the solutions.

## Create an upward spiral for achieving *one-to-100* goals

You must create an upward spiral in the process of achieving your *one-to-100* goals. It is not so difficult for an individual employee to generate momentum toward his/her own goal. The organization as a whole must do the same to seize the current and ride with it. There is a phase when many members feel "the wind is blowing favorably" or "this is the decisive moment." Those organizations that pursue the *one-to-100* goals often experience such moments.

When we encounter such a situation, we must take the plunge riding the wave, because we never know when the next chance will be. It is scary for sure to jump on such an upward spiral. Especially those who have little experience would feel very anxious. On the other hand, those who have taken the plunge many times in the past know that they can get to the new stage by riding such a wave, therefore, they find it easy to do so.

When you jump into the current, there is a moment when all the participants share the feeling of unison. It feels as if their bodies are floating up together. At such a moment, everyone's levels of abstraction are raised as well. From then on, you can expect concrete changes to start occurring. Such changes in the organization are widened perspectives, ease of generating ideas, better handling of problems, not being afraid of failures, etc. These reflect the qualitative changes happening in the organization. These can happen in any type of work. You may personally recall similar changes that you have experienced before.

What is happening in the brains of the participants at the time is having a shared sense of reality. If you have a strong sense of reality in what you imagine in your brain, you can also share it with others to see. As an organization rallies around the common goal, the participants start feeling as if they see the same image together. This is the timing when B2C (business to consumer) companies start producing new innovative products and B2B (business to business) companies creating ground-breaking business models.

This is the state where you are locked onto the goal and you don't hear noises around you. This should not end up as a one-time event. The key is how to sustain the momentum for a long time.

Incidentally, this is the stage where coaching is most needed. While the coach plays an important role in any stage, this junction is the one where organizations find it most difficult to maintain the momentum on their own.

Now, I will explain the three fundamental powers necessary for mobilizing an organization. You will need them in this order: first, *power to instill*; then, *power to set an example*; and finally, *power to trust others and wait*.

## Power to instill: injection

### 1. Penetration of the vision is indispensable for the organization to work autonomously.

---

You start by *instilling the message*. The president is the one who does this. The message gives a sense of reality to the comfort zone in the desired state. When the message is instilled, the receivers' brain is locked onto the two world – one is the desired state itself and the other is the receivers' own world moving toward the goal. The latter is a sort of meditative state where they are visualizing themselves achieving the goal. This state feels like the brain is feeling a rush of enthusiasm yet maintaining an objective view. They are fascinated but they are not losing themselves. In the world of Kabuki, Japanese performance art, there is a state which is called "noru (flow)." This is a technique to stay mindful while intoxicated. The state that the company is experiencing may be similar to what the Kabuki players are feeling.

## 2. Passionate enthusiasm, not reasoning, mobilizes people.

Passionate enthusiasm is inevitably spread to people. However, it has a weakness, too. It does not have sustaining power. The fervor of enthusiasm can cool down quickly. Thus, relying on passionate enthusiasm alone is no good. Nevertheless, we should remember to rekindle it at times.

## 3. An organization that thinks from the future.

Let me introduce a company in Saitama prefecture, Japan, with about 100 employees. One of this company's characteristics is that all employees are forward-looking. Therefore, their reflection is carried out positively as well. Everyone is in the mode of generating new ideas. They always remember their customers' viewpoints and work for customer delight. When this company announces hiring, it attracts a huge number of candidates. It is noteworthy that their employee turnover rate is extremely low. Naturally, their business keeps steadily growing. You may be able to imagine the strength of the company that naturally thinks from the future.

## 4. Draw out the employees' talents while maintaining the unifying force.

In this regard, the important thing is how to have the employees stay with the company. Of course, when the company itself and the job contents are attractive, employees would work hard. Even so, there are times when people change their view of life. They may feel driven by the thought "I should be able to do better," or they may become dissatisfied by the limitations that are imposed on them due to their role or business. Thus, the employees may find reasons to quit their jobs at any time. Is there anything we can do to prevent this from happening?

## 5. Two pillars of unity – people and vision.

Let's suppose that you focus on the employees' talents and elevate their self-efficacy. These are good things to do. However, if you do so without careful attention, the employees' focus may move outward, and the risk of losing them will increase. You need to be mindful about which way you want them to grow. Otherwise, they will grow out of the company.

If you are not careful, in organizations where autonomy starts working, a centrifugal force starts working at a certain stage. The employees who shine will be attractive targets for outside recruiters. Of course, it is not a bad thing for those individual employees. Even though this may sometimes be unavoidable, if possible, you want them to grow in the same direction that your company is heading.

What can you do to maintain cohesiveness and unity in such an environment? What is helpful is indeed the personality and attractiveness of the president and management. It includes a down-to-earth approach such as interacting occasionally at a personal level with the employees.

Of course, the basic approach is to show them the company's Gold Vision while paying attention to the individual employee's goal. The personality and attractiveness of the top management and the company's vision are like two wheels of a cart. They should not be skewed to one side but should be balanced.

## 6. A president's arbitrary decisions and executions can cause others to pull them down.

---

A president's arbitrary execution generates many dream killers. Careful attention is needed.

From the viewpoint of employees, the company's drastic change is threatening, even to their very existence. In their subconscious mind, they would be thinking, "The company is changing so fast. No way I can catch up with it. Sooner or later, I might lose my job." Any organization that goes through drastic changes does experience this strong force pulling them backward, and this unconscious thought is directly connected to the mass generation of dream killers. It is challenging to deal with the dream killers, as they sometimes masquerade as supporters of the organization.

While they are telling the president, "It's a great idea," outwardly, they may obstruct the efforts inwardly. They may not be conscious of this behavior. Sometimes, the president himself/herself is moving forward too aggressively becoming his/her own dream killer.

Dream killers exist outside the company, too. Those who have been cooperative can change their attitude. For example, the outside directors and advisors whom the president has trusted could pull the organization's efforts down. More than anybody else, those who would pull down the organization are the corporate lawyers and accountants. The laws and accounting that they have dealt with represent "the past" itself. Their professions by definition may be said to be furthest from futuristic thinking. Furthermore, they can lose their jobs, as the organization grows. The lawyers and accountants suitable for companies with sales of 1 million are different from those for companies with sales of 100 million. They know it; thus, they unconsciously try to stop the transformation.

What can you do? First, don't rush it. You cannot get upset even if they pull you down because of your arbitrary decisions and executions. Introspect if you are smashing through it. If you recognize that you are rushing, you should consciously be in tune with the pace of the people around you.

At the same time, you need to develop supporters inside the company. If necessary, you might consider inviting others from outside the company. Keep it in mind, though, there is a risk that they might betray you. In any event, the most important thing is that you keep showing the transformed image of the company to the employees and supporters.

## Power to set an example: Being a role model

The next topic is *the power to set an example* or *be a role model*. Those who set the tone are the president and the leaders of the company.

## 1. You show it through your practice.

You present yourself trying to move to your new comfort zone. You, the president, may not look cool, because it entails lots of struggles. Many of my clients deal with this condition saying, "It's hard, it's hard." This is important because the organization will not change unless the employees feel the president, too, is struggling and working hard. Naturally, it is hard, because it requires you to make a break from the past and acquire new habits. I do understand your sentiment of wanting to hide your struggles. However, I say this is not something to hide. The struggles to move to the new comfort zone are something to be shared with all employees.

In my previous book, I touched upon the condition called *comfort-zone sickness*. When people are trying to move to their new comfort zone, many of them experience fatigue, sickness, and stomachache. I call these conditions *comfort-zone sickness*. Since this sickness is something to be experienced together, it does not make sense for the president to hide it. The best way is to learn to face it together with the employees.

## 2. The meaning of sharing struggles.

There is a reason for the president's struggles to be seen. By realizing that the president is a human after all, the employees are more likely to share the comfort zone. There may be presidents who feel better having the employees think that the top management is special. Unfortunately, if this state persists, they cannot expect their employees to manifest their maximum potential. It is because the employees are intimidated. The president is the one who loses if the employees are overawed.

Thus, it is better to give up superficial coolness. However, it depends on his/her goal. If the goal is to pursue the president's coolness, he/she should not have any hesitation to do so. In such a case, though, it would be difficult to strive for a *one-to-100* goal, but I am not trying to stop it.

## 3. It is okay to fail.

"It is okay to fail," is a phrase often spoken to the employees. I dare to present it to CEOs, too. If CEOs are challenging new things, they, too, can fail. There is no law that CEOs cannot fail. Wouldn't you agree with me that a CEO, who is overcoming the grim reality of the situation not going as hoped, together with the employees, is cool?

## 4. Improve the top management's caliber.

Three factors constitute the president's caliber. They are *the strength and worthiness of the cause, the scale of the goal,* and *the power of self-efficacy.* Among the factors, one can change by oneself is the size of the goal. To grow the president's caliber, he/she must enlarge the goal. For this purpose, the president should associate with those of higher caliber. Rather than staying in his/her own office, he/she must actively go out. Rather than taking on lots of work, the president has to delegate it to his/her subordinates.

## 5. President's choices: "Wants to grow with the company?" or "Wants to grow rich?"

Let's be honest. It is not a bad thing if the president himself/herself wants to be rich. If he/she wants to secure monetary gain by listing stocks, it is good to let his/her intention be known upfront. It is also natural that he/she wants to get more rewards by making the business bigger.

In addition, the president starts thinking about the way for both he/she and the employees to grow rich. Under such a president, those employees who also want to be rich are likely to gather. In this circumstance, it is possible to get better results.

On the other hand, if the president wants to grow with the company, he/she should bring it to the forefront. Under such a president, those employees who gather are also motivated to grow. In this circumstance, too, you can expect better results.

"Wanting to grow with the company" and "wanting to grow rich" are both factors for growth. In actual business management, those companies belonging to the former often have a goal of contributing to everyone's development, whereas the latter companies set a goal of contributing to society's wealth. It is not a question of which is better. The concern here is to choose the direction that is most suitable for you.

Incidentally, there was a time I contemplated the reasons for working. Firstly, the basic reason is "work for wealth."

According to Abraham Maslow's hierarchy of needs, it corresponds to *physiological needs* and *safety needs*. The next reason is "work for the meaning of existence," which relates to Maslow's *belongingness and love needs* and *esteem needs*. Then the final reason is "work for growth," which is similar to Maslow's *self-actualization needs*.

I believe there are three stages of why people work. From the bottom up, they work wanting to become secure and grow rich, wanting to find meaning in their lives, and then wanting to grow. Among the three reasons for work, the highest is their own growth. However, there is no problem whatever the reason why people work. Any job includes all three factors. The president needs to choose one of the three and strongly drive it in the organization. Then you can expect the employees who align with the cause to come together.

## 6. Your behavior is always watched.

The way the president lives determines the image of the company. Indeed, he/she is the role model. This point should be kept in mind. What the president says and does reflects the company standards, such as handling the expense account, employee interactions, attitude toward information management, and work approach. In a company where the president uses his/her power to harass, so do other employees. If the president is involved in sexual harassment, it will be a common practice in the company.

**Figure 19: "Reasons to work" and Maslow's "Hierarchy of needs"**

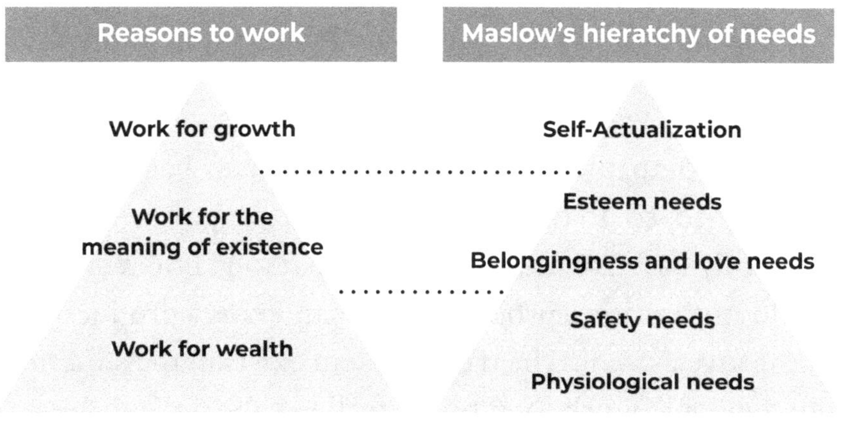


Source: KAZUYOSHI HISANO AND CONOWAY, INC.

## 7. Organizations with high self-efficacy respect legal compliance.

Those organizations that strongly believe that they can achieve the goal honor the rules. Those organizations with shaky compliance lack confidence. Negligence of the rules is a function of low confidence.

There was a time when the news reported one cover-up incident after another. Without exception, companies that were involved in acts of dishonesty seemed to have a lack of confidence. In brief, they do things dishonestly, because they worry that they may not be able to win. If they maintain the comfort zone, where they can think that they can win next time even if they lose this time, there is no room for dishonesty.

## 8. President sets the company standards for how and how much to work.

In the age of work-style reforms, the key is *want-to*.

In the company where the president lives based on his/her *want-to*, so do the employees. If the organization functions truly based on *want-to*, somewhat long hours of work would not create a problem. You can expect productivity to improve as well. The true problem exists in the situation where people work long hours feeling they *have to*.

## 9. How do we not lose talented individuals?

When you hire talented individuals, your assumption needs to be that you never know when they will leave your company. Thus, you should be grateful for the fact that they are working for you now. This way of dealing with them is the key in the long run so as not to lose them. You must continue thinking about the role in which each individual can shine the most and presenting the way to utilize his/her potential to the maximum.

In a company that pursues a *one-to-100* goal, workforce movement occurs to a certain extent. It may be likened to a professional sports team. While you assume the possibility of your excellent employees moving to another company, you need to have them put their fullest efforts into each game and each season.

### Power to trust and wait: Empowerment

The third power to mobilize the organization is *the power to trust and wait.*

## 1. Begin with the "ready assist" mode.

Of course, there is no need to leave everything up to your subordinates. You can trust them and let them do part of the work. It requires time to get used to the condition for both you and them. It is desirable to first make this state the comfort zone. One way to start delegating your work to another is to create your absence for a day or for a week at a time. The other way may be to delegate your work for a limited period.

Small failures should be welcome in fact. The person who made a mistake would be nervous, but those who delegated should remain calm about the situation as expected.

## 2. Delegate and then wait.

Don't hurry, but wait, should be understood as the only way to nurture people. This is not difficult to understand at all if you think of it.

Let's suppose you plant the seeds of morning glory. What will you do? You might water them from time to time, but all you mainly do is just to wait. It is the same with raising a child; we have no other choice but to wait.

However, to stay calm while waiting, you need to have a Plan B. You need to think ahead about what you will do when things go wrong and share some of it with those who are concerned. Set a deadline and wait.

## 3. Belief enables performance.

If you think that someone may not be able to do, you should not delegate your work to them. The most important thing is that they feel that they will be able to do it. You need to have them understand the concept of self-efficacy and experience it.

You might say, "Psychology has the term 'self-efficacy,' and belief in yourself is said to be necessary for success and achieving results. You may not have the confidence now but know that if you feel that you can't do it, the probability of failure goes up. As I feel confident about you, I am leaving it up to you. I want you to feel that you can do it. If you have any difficulty, come to me. We will think what we can do together."

You may visualize the above as a scene from a drama or cartoon book. As a leader, I believe, you have the time to take the role of the boss and carry it out. Of course, you may want to adapt the line to your liking. Nevertheless, it is a good idea to talk to your subordinates in this manner at times.

## 4. How do you delegate at critical junctures?

When you delegate, the assumption is that it is okay to fail. Otherwise, the person who is delegated cannot take a bold step. Thus, when a failure is critical and would result in disaster, you should not delegate. Delegation is for human resources development. Regarding nurturing people, you do not need to gamble at all. What you need is a plan, and readiness to take responsibility in case of failure. As a type of insurance, you might want to assign someone you trust to support the person to whom you have delegated the work.

## 5. How do you handle it when you feel you can't let it continue?

There may be a time when you feel that this can't go as it is now. However, let's not pull back right away from the work you delegated to your subordinates. If you did, they would hate you for the rest of their lives.

When you need to confirm your feeling that something is not going well, you can use the method of *Feedforward*. You can ask how the person is planning to do it and grasp the situation in his/her answer. When the situation is bad, you will hear a confused answer, which does not make sense. While you maintain your attitude of support that the other person feels easy to get some help, you should encourage him/her to back off.

The other situation may be that the person you delegated to has no idea that he/she is in a critical situation. It is desirable to have that person recognize it on his/her own. If it does not happen, you may need to intervene to convey the situation. Ultimately, it is your responsibility, and you are the one who assigned that person to the work. However, you don't know until you try. Therein lies the difficulty.

## 6. What will you do when the above does not work?

If it is so difficult, you need to take the work back. The priority should be according to the urgency of the tasks required. The time to get it back is a little before it becomes too late. You need to be careful not to wait until it is too late. To avoid your judgment becoming too late, communication is vital. Furthermore, those who delegate also need to maintain attentiveness. It is like the on-call duty of a surgeon, who is out of an operating room but standing by for an emergency.

It is important to clearly inform the person why you judged that it is difficult for the person to carry on. There is no guarantee that the person will get it, nevertheless, it is a crucial process. Keep in mind that this process must take place before the transition, no matter how busy you are, not after everything is done.

If the person agrees, you might consider moving him/her to another job within the project, rather than letting him/

her go, for the next opportunity. While you continue communicating, you will find the next opportunity for him/her.

## 7. Courage to accept the results – self-efficacy.

When you delegate, it is up to the boss to take the responsibility. Even if the results are unfavorable, you must be able to say, "Don't worry, leave it up to me." You do not need to worry. You may stumble, but it is not the end. If you have the self-efficacy that you can manage it, you will have the courage to take it back

### Important things for not leaving the organization behind

I have already mentioned what happens when top management goes ahead in his/her way. When the top of the organization runs alone, the organization is left behind. That's the way it is. Naturally, if this continues, the organization can break up. What can you do then? The basic condition here is to wait. At the same time, the president has to have his/her subordinate leaders go to the front line so as not to create too much of a gap between the top management and the organization. The president himself/herself must always keep looking at the goal. Thus, the president needs his/her leaders' support to involve the front line so that they are not left behind.

# Magic words to transform resistance into support in one week

Are there really such magic words to transform resistance into support? Yes, there are. As a professional coach, I have been using the following phrases with success in my practice:

"I would like to have your advice."
"What do you think we can do?"
"Will you help me?"

I hope you will try these words. The key is to deal with the person with your readiness to work shoulder-to-shoulder to deal with the impact of the change. One week may be a little exaggeration but I assure you of the effects. This is an approach that I have been using since my junior high school days. I don't think these are anything new, but those who haven't tried it will be surprised by its effectiveness.

## Coming closer to your employees

You cannot run your business without employees. Once you realize that you are not the only one who is carrying out your business, you will value the people around you more. This realization will make you feel a love for your employees.

I once asked a president who had troubles with his wife. "How often do you say, 'Thank you,' to her?" His answer was as I expected. He said, "I rarely do." I replied, "Really? But it's quite important."

Without a partner, things do not go around. Thus, feelings such as gratitude and love are a natural consequence. When the levels of abstraction are low, the president would only see things from his point of view. Let's raise the levels of abstraction so that we can care about the employees and suppliers. This is a key point not to be forgotten for a company to grow. The readiness to take on challenges can be interpreted as your desire to achieve the goal. Here, too, proceeding with *want-to* rather than *have-to* is important.

## Handling an employee with a mental health issue

How do you cope with the case when an employee faces burnout? Let us first recognize that this is the result of the overload, and that no one should be blamed.

When this situation arises in a team of five or six people, it is quite a burden to the team. Their spirit will be low even when they go to lunch. As a result, they can hardly do anything. The team may find it difficult to communicate with the person with the problem. The situation will worsen with time; the person comes to work late and leaves early, furthermore, he/she becomes frequently absent.

It is important not to think you can manage the case on your own. Rather, you should not be hesitant to seek professional help. At any rate, you need to do the best you can, and doing so is for your benefit as well in the long run.

When such a problem occurs, you may not know exactly to what extent you should get involved. A situation could arise where you may need to accompany the person to a hospital. You need to maintain the attitude of welcoming consultation at any time.

The manager of the person often tends to blame himself/herself in such a case. However, this does not solve the problem. Of course, if there is an element of abuse of power as the underlying cause, he/she needs to reflect on this sincerely. In the current social environment, it is rare to see such a case in which the cause-and-effect relationship is clear and straightforward. We need to be prepared for it as unavoidable.

When we face the situation, the leader and other people associated may feel disappointed, but this is inevitable. As leaders, we need to incorporate this type of problem as a possible future scenario and adjust our expectation level accordingly.

## Clarify emotional and monetary rewards.

There are two types of rewards: emotional and monetary. During the period of rapid economic growth in Japan, there was a culture where one could say "The reward for good work is another good assignment." However, such an approach today would be criticized as "exploitation" of employees. Nevertheless, I believe that people should be given opportunities to enjoy their work more.

In terms of emotional rewards, I believe that people will get full benefits through working on what they *want*. The heart is content when we work toward our *want-to* goals. Also, we need to be mindful of human-to-human connections.

As much as possible, we ensure a work environment where the employees can enjoy working toward their goals because good human relations are important factors for emotional rewards.

Having that said, monetary rewards are important, of course. Naturally, it is a part of management's job to squarely face this issue and strive for enhanced satisfaction.

It is not that people feel enjoyment when they grow, rather they can grow as they work joyously, despite difficult challenges.

# How to Increase Management Performance For Hundred-Fold Growth:

## Shift Your Comfort Zone

**Feel a sense of reality in the comfort zone
of the world of 100**

In the prologue of this book, the concept of *one-to-100* management was introduced. In this chapter, we will discuss the *one-to-100* thinking and the *one-to-100* ideas that support such management.

I define *the one-to-100 thinking* as a system of thinking that enables *one-to-100* management, and *the one-to-100 ideas* as an approach that especially emphasizes *intuition* in *the one-to-100 thinking*.

It may take some time to turn one into 100, but it is not difficult to do. What's important is how to cultivate the *intuition* that makes *one-to-100* possible.

If you are in a state of being in which you can experience the comfort zone of the *one-to-100* world, your brain will try to realize the world of 100 without hesitation.

Note that I purposely say, "the comfort zone of the world of 100." It may sound a minor point, but it's important not to "feel the world of 100 is real," but to "feel the comfort zone of the world of 100 is real." It may be difficult to feel the world of 100 itself, but on the contrary, it is easy to have a sense of reality in the comfort zone of the world of 100. It's because the comfort zone is the world where you are in. It may be difficult to imagine everything in the world, but you should be able to enhance the reality of your comfort zone by imagining your surroundings.

And it's the RAS (reticular activating system) I described in the prologue that will work to bring the world of *one-to-100* to life. The brain uses the RAS to collect information and make decisions almost simultaneously. The important activities in management are judgment and action. Since judgment has been completed by RAS, the next step is to take action.

To make this an organizational process, I created Goal Theory, Feedforward Theory, and Cause Theory.

## Achieve the goal through *one-to-100* thinking with management by all

Management with *one-to-100* thinking is, in other words, *management by all*. In the case of a company with 5 to 10 employees, if the top management has the *one-to-100* thinking, the results will come quickly. However, when it comes to a company with a scale of a few hundred people, no matter how hard the top person works with *one-to-100* thinking, it will be very difficult to get quick results. The only way to become an organization that can realize hundred-fold growth is to get everyone, from top management to front-line members into hundred-fold thinking. Then it will naturally become an organization that can realize *one-to-100*. It's not just the top management, but every member's intuition will be sharpened to move forward toward the goal.[42]

A similar state is seen in a strong team fighting in a team sports competition. All members have a strong sense of reality for "winning." However, a game in the world of sports is different from that in the business world.

Even if every member of your team has a well-honed intuition for the goal, if the competitor team does the same, the result will be unpredictable. In such a case, the team that has a deeper penetration of the *one-to-100* thinking and is superior in technique as well as physical strength will be a winner.

---

42  Hisano states that when we set a high goal our intuition will give us the necessary ideas to attain it. – Editor

Also, even if you achieved *one-to-100*, it's not meaningful if it was transient. The best situation will be that many people in the organization experience the essence of *one-to-100* over and over, not just once, and become capable of sustainably supporting the state by themselves.

Inevitably, both people and companies hit a plateau in the process of growth. For a variety of reasons, such as changing customers, changing competitive relationships, government regulations, and organizational rigidities; the previous model will no longer work in the next stage. If you don't make it through this plateau, you won't be able to move on to the next stage.[43]

Management by all, with a *one-to-100* mindset, involves both top management leading the organization and the organization functioning in a bottom-up manner. From top to bottom, everyone in the organization can feel the reality of the comfort zone in the world of the goal of 100.

Additionally, the *one-to-100* leader must uphold the Gold Vision while also being attentive to the goals of the members. He/she works tirelessly to ensure that the organization and individuals can identify shared goals.

When that becomes the norm, the members will find their place in the organization and feel comfortable working there.

Research by Google[44] has revealed that "increasing psychological safety improves team performance and creativity." I confirm this from my experience as a professional coach.

---

43  This is especially true the time with the world of the "virus." But look at this "virus" as an opportunity to foster change for you. – Editor

44  https://rework.withgoogle.com/print/guides/5721312655835136/

Management encourages members to *set goals* daily and supports them to increase their *efficacy*. This makes it easier for members to be in the comfort zone of the *one-to-100* world.

Figure 20: "1 to 100 thinking" enables "management by all." The goals will sharpen intuition of all the organization members.

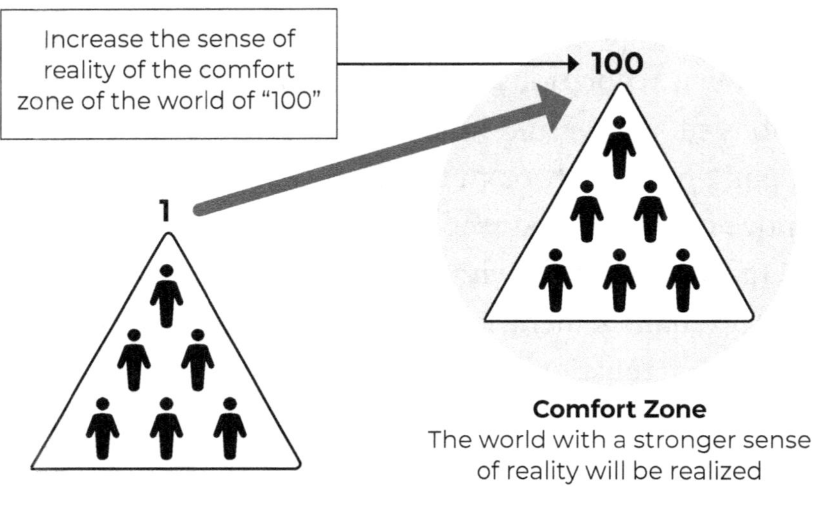


Source: KAZUYOSHI HISANO AND CONOWAY, INC.

Of course, you also encourage your team members to imagine the "good things" that they can experience when 100 is realized. This is the role of a leader in *one-to-100* management.

As I already explained, a company that can achieve *one-to-100* has the capability to grow continually. Therefore, it won't get stagnant. However, if you don't renew your goals, sooner or later your growth will end. Also, you will eventually be asked this question with the actual number,

"Now that 100 times is achieved, are you going to aim for 300 times next?" However, as the next stage of *one-to-100*, whether to aim for 300 should be determined by each organization. This is because all employees, including the CEO, need to think about *what they really want to do*.

### How to turn a one million company into 100 million company (theory and practice)

Finally, we have come to the part of *How to turn a one million company into a 100 million company*. I will explain by dividing this into *theory* and *practice*. I have talked about the theory from many angles, but I can summarize it in one line as follows.

### [Theory]
### All members have moved to a state of mind that takes 100 million for granted.

---

Now on to the practical part. Let's express it in one line too.

### [Practice 1]
### Sharpen the intuition of all members.

---

We discussed "sharpening the intuition of all members" in more detail in the previous section. The important thing here is not to think small. If you think "We are a small company," your actions will only get smaller. So, what should we do? You can visualize your company as a big company. Then I would recommend you have a relationship with a person in a big company. It doesn't matter if you are a customer or a vendor in the relationship. It is okay to just be friends.

There are players in the company who have been given various positions, including the CEO. Among them, the levels that should actively utilize *the power to involve and move people* are the CEO, executives, and department heads. The CEO and executives should go out and take on the role of increasing their comfort zone in various social interactions. Specifically, as mentioned above, they should build relationships with managers and executives of big companies and experience the world of 100 million, one billion, and ten billion.

Department heads are expected to follow suit. A department head is a potential future executive. If the active department head is unable to think like an executive, the company will not be able to grow. Ideally, I would like them to think and come up with ideas at the level of a CEO.

On the other hand, section managers and below must first fulfill their duties under the vision instilled by the organization as a priority. Of course, they need to broaden their horizons as they move up in the position.

## [Practice 2]
## Create a chunk of 20 to 30 million.

It's not easy to reach 100 million in a single leap. It is necessary to establish a chunk of 20 to 30 million on the roadmap.

So, how can you create a chunk of 20 to 30 million? This is where specific product or service development and marketing/sales are needed. The core of this book is *one-to-100 thinking* and *one-to-100 ideas*, so I won't go into the details of these specific business techniques for product and service development here. However, what I would like to tell you is that imitation and copying someone will never be able to create such a chunk.

There is something called the "Blue Ocean Strategy.[45]" It defines the existing competitive market as the "Red Ocean" and advises us to open up the untapped Blue Ocean market. Naturally, if you imitate what someone else has made, it becomes a competition. It will lead to a price war and increase operating costs. As a result, you may end up in a situation where *one-to-100* was achieved but not the profit.

We need to develop something truly novel. You may say, "It will never be as easy as you say. That's what I am struggling for." Let me answer that. *Gold Vision* will help you build the novel products that you are trying to develop. As I already mentioned, *Gold Vision* can enable you to increase

---

45 **Blue ocean strategy** is the simultaneous pursuit of differentiation and low cost to open up a new market space and create new demand. It is about creating and capturing uncontested market space, thereby making the competition irrelevant.

the levels of abstraction. We have many techniques and practices to help you do that. As your levels of abstraction increase, you will certainly be able to think creatively."

Here we must note that large companies do not suffer from lack of growth. Most large enterprises and old enterprises suffer from stagnation. They simply cannot innovate. The biggest concern of the CEOs of these companies is making their companies more innovative. No textbook strategy will force your company to become more innovative. There has to be a fundamental change in the thinking. Here we offer *Gold Vision* as a method for innovation.

Some companies like Microsoft have been good at reinventing themselves. In the 80s, Microsoft started with operating systems. In the 90s, they moved to networking. In 2000, they came out with Office. In 2010, they offered Cloud systems. Nowadays, they give away their highest-selling product Windows, for free because they are making so much more in their cloud business. Windows today contains one-time rival Linux as a subsystem; Microsoft Cloud is running on Linux. Of course, sometimes they made wrong bets too.

In the 2000s, they wanted to enter into hardware. They produced a mouse, keyboards, and then mobile phones. They continued this with their Surface tablets. All failed to become big businesses. But that is part of their challenge. On the other hand, Xbox took off as another business and grew massively. If a company does not move its comfort zone, it becomes irrelevant. Microsoft did this by embracing Linux and Opensource recently and moving its focus to delivering cloud services. Do you still remember Blackberry or Nokia? When they were the market leaders in mobile phones Samsung and Apple were not even in the market.

## If you don't shift your comfort zone, your organization won't grow

I once attended a networking event. The CEO of a company with annual sales of 100 million and the CEO of a company with annual sales of 1 million were having a conversation. But they were not talking about the same thing in their conversation. The reason for the gap was obvious. The comfort zones of the two CEOs were completely different.

For example, the company with annual sales of 1 million had 8 employees, including the CEO, while the company with annual sales of 100 million has 400 employees.

The two companies were doing very different things in terms of employee training and management. With 8 employees, you can run a family business, but in a company with 400 employees, a family business will likely be impossible.

The CEO of the 100 million company has created an HR appraisal system and determines salaries for the employees based on the evaluations. However, the CEO of the 1 million company makes decisions based on his subjectivity. These two companies are in the same manufacturing industry, but the manufacturing of the 1 million company and that of the 100 million company are in different markets and are serving different customers. Their product profile is also different.

The 1 million company manufactures products on a made-to-order basis, while the 100 million company manufactures on a make-to-stock basis at its factory.

They may be the same in terms of the position of CEO, but the world that they see is completely different.

If the CEO of the 1 million company wants to become the CEO of a 100 million company, the first thing that he needs to do is to transform his mindset. Furthermore, the employees must also change their mindset to "we are working for a 100 million company."

The following three steps are necessary for an organization to work autonomously:

1. Show a vision and instill a mindset.
2. The top management leads by example.
3. Leave it to the field and wait.

This will increase the comfort zone and increase the company's sales. As you and your organization begin to grow, your relationships with those around you will also change. The challenge and burden that had felt comfortable when you were earning 1 million in annual sales gradually change, and you feel "comfortable" with that of the company which earns 5 million in annual sales. You start to spend more time on dinner and golf with CEOs or leaders who are running businesses of 5 million in annual sales. Eventually, you begin to feel more "comfortable" spending time with such people than with your former companions. In this way, you become accustomed to your new comfort zone. A change in the comfort zone of the CEO changes the comfort zone of executives and leaders, and the comfort zone of the entire organization will also change. As a result, the comfort zone of the members also rises, and employees begin to make extra efforts and take on more challenging tasks on their own, even if the CEO doesn't give instructions at every step.

In this way, the elevation of the comfort zone of each member is directly related to the improvement of the organization's performance, and the organization will be closer to a company with annual sales of 100 million.

The members start saying "We want to provide better products and better services. We want our customers to be more satisfied," and at the same time, they will start to think "I want to receive higher compensation. I want to live a more prosperous life. I want to feel a deeper sense of accomplishment."

It is the role of the CEO and leaders to make members feel comfortable in such a high comfort zone, to make them envision the future, and to make them take it for granted.

## The limitations of financial incentives

Financial incentives alone will not sustain performance. It may sound obvious, but let's clarify this point. One of the most important things in the management of a company is to create an atmosphere of liveliness and joy at work. You could say, "It is to create an organization where people are willing to work hard." In creating such an organization, it is the balance wheel that plays the role of an "engine." The balance wheel depicts the sense of reality of the comfort zone on the goal side. It creates the energy to get there.

Again, in thinking about the balance wheel, you need to focus on the goals of the organization and all the individuals. When you find the point that is shared by the two, the output power of the engine will go up significantly.

The individual's balance wheel is easy to understand, but the organization's balance wheel might need a little explanation. People often ask me, "I understand the concept of the *Balance Wheel*, but what should be put inside?" If you are not yet involved in management, it may be difficult to see this.

**Figure 21: Balance wheel of an organization.**

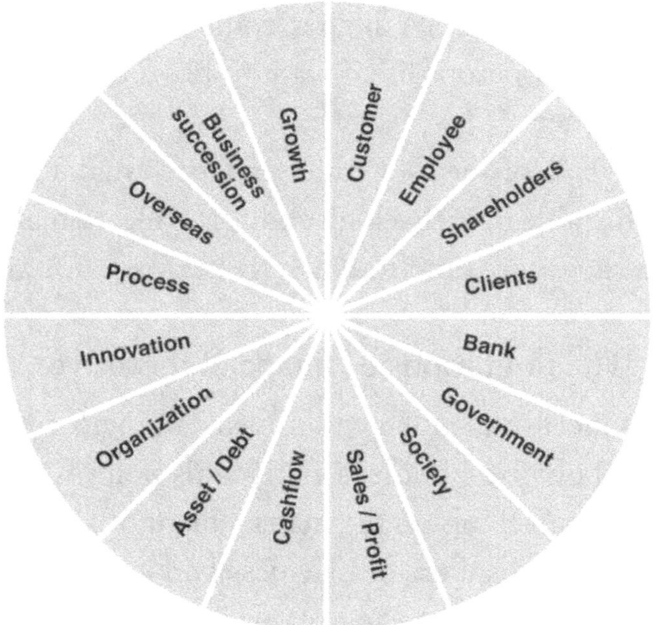


Source: KAZUYOSHI HISANO AND CONOWAY, INC.

Let me give you some examples. Stakeholders, such as customers, employees, shareholders, banks, government, local governments, local communities, etc. Finance items, such as sales, profit, cash flow, assets, and liabilities, as well as the items that stem from management's concerns, such as organization, innovation, and process.

If you list these items, you can quickly find 10 to 20 elements. For each item, there is usually one or more goals. If you combine this with an individual's balance wheel, you should be able to find a point where the balance wheel of the organization and the individual match.

## When an organization has a sudden awakening

When I am discussing training for a company, I am sometimes asked "How many people should participate in the training?" My response is, "If a minimum of 30% of all employees understand the hundred-fold mindset, it would be possible to transform a company. However, with anything below 20%, this will be very difficult."

When I am confronted with this question, I always ask, "How many managers do you have?" Let's take a company of 100 people for example. There is only one CEO for sure. There are several executive officers. When it comes to the managing staff below them, there are probably a dozen or so. So far, they account for less than 20%. Then I ask, "Can't you also add a few from those who have leadership potential?" Eventually, the figure adds up to nearly 30%. That's about the percentage you need to transform your organization.

Those who were trained begin to have a ripple effect on their surroundings and their comfort zone begins to shift, slowly in the beginning, but gradually change in the organization will accelerate.

Organizations are interesting. When the members of an organization are united, it changes into totally a different creature. Once the ripple effect begins to spread from the managing staff, the number of people who think "maybe we can do this" starts to increase, and the number of people who think "it is impossible" decreases. After that, the critical point comes.

When the percentage of the people who think "we can do this" reaches enough, what happens is that it turns into literally a different company (or organization) overnight. I have witnessed such "awakening" many times in the past.

The first thing that changes in an awakened organization is its "language." The *organizational* version of "self-talk" is called "corporate talk." The old "corporate talk" that is in the old comfort zone is replaced by the new "corporate talk" that drives the organization and its members toward the realization of their goals. When you are in this state, you are fully on a growth trajectory.

### It takes time because you think it will

This is very true in the case of practicing the *one-to-100* mindset. Here you need to make a distinction between the change in mind (brain and heart) and the change in the real world.

It certainly takes time to achieve the *one-to-100* growth physically. Typically, this takes a minimum of four years or so. But a change in the mind (brain and heart) is another matter. The comfort zone is about the mind (brain and heart). Change happens instantly. It is a different matter from an organization's actual growth.

However, sustaining the changes in the mind that occurred in an instant is also a different matter. The mind may go back to its original state. Therefore, the shift of the comfort zone needs to be repeated to make it permanent. By consciously increasing the sense of reality on the goal side, you will make the comfort zone in the 100 world a natural state for you.

Let me repeat this: physical growth of *one-to-100* needs time. However, the mind (brain and heart) can change in an instant. The key is to firmly establish the change and to turn it into action.

## If you grow up too fast, you will miss your step

A "no rush" attitude is essential in the process of growth. The brain has an interesting quality. When you are in a hurry, it will be easy to overlook things. Eventually, it will be faster to follow the process of growth by reminding yourself, "Slowly, slowly."

There is no need to be concerned because the results will follow. Above all, it is important to keep your efficacy high and not disrupt your state of mind focused on your goal. When the brain is in a good state, the landscape can seem to be in slow motion. There is an expression in the baseball world that players say, "The ball looks as if it stops." This is very similar.

It isn't just sports, it's the same for work. When you are focused and in "the zone," it may feel like a long time has passed, but sometimes it hasn't. The *one-to-100* management is management by all. When more of your employees can spend their time in this state, the growth from there will be fast.

## All members have the mindset of a 100 million company

When members feel "It is achievable," they will be drawn to that direction. The *one-to-100* management is management by all. Top management needs to manage the company based on *one-to-100* thinking. That said, it is not necessary for every single employee in the field to fully acquire the *one-to-100* thinking. If they master only part of it, the whole organization will be leaning toward *one-to-100*. Just a little bit at a time, you can instill the *one-to-100* thinking in the whole. Accumulation of "little bits" will drive the organizational change. As a result, it will be easier for the senior management to navigate the operation. In *one-to-100* management, it is strictly forbidden for the management to make statements such as, "My subordinates don't understand it anyway," or "Our employees are not at that level." That would never be true.

## Review the business model and thoroughly focus on "reproducibility"

What sells explosively is "a new concept that no one has ever seen before." It doesn't matter if it's a product or a service.

You need to commit to reproducibility after you come up with a novel concept. Reproducibility will need to be achieved with consistency. CEOs are concerned with this process. Do you remember CEOs' concerns? The fourth one was "process." Building a process and keeping costs down while maintaining quality is reproducibility.

One of my MBA classmates had expertise in a unique area. She was an executive officer in charge of a call center at a prestigious company. In other words, she was an expert in customer relations and a professional who developed the call center staff. Her job was to present what it should be, decide a concept, create a process, and implement it. After that, training follows. This will help the staff to grow. She had complete mastery over this series of systems. She worked at several top-tier companies in multiple industries and built call centers with a proven track record. This is an example of a high level of reproducibility.

It is important to pursue a novel concept. On the other hand, you will lose everything if the company goes out of business. The answer is simple. You should run after two hares.

Here again, the power of the unconscious can be relied on. While refining the process and doing the daily tasks, keep the unconscious working at full capacity. The unconscious will always look out for innovative concepts. If you set your goals properly, your unconscious will work that way.

While consolidating the foundation of management, do not become entirely occupied with it. Instead, focus on creating original products and services by setting goals that go beyond the status quo. So long as you effectively harness your subconscious, this is something you can achieve.

## Thoroughly improve the quality of your products and services

In any company, to "choose a customer" is one of the essences of management. It is also important not to deal with customers you don't like. However, the company that achieves the *one-to-100* is a little different. You need to be "the customer's choice."

In the process of achieving the *one-to-100*, the company will grow together with the customers who nurture the company itself. It is the customer who gives legitimacy to the company's attitude toward *one-to-100*. Legitimacy here refers to having people think, "This is the company that will do this for me."

When a company that breaks industry conventions and grows with the user's perspective is touted as a "standard-bearer of innovation," there is always customer support behind it. Customers are also brand ambassadors. It's important to create a state like this.

A recent example is Netflix. Newcomers to the online video distribution service are also following suit. Netflix has now become synonymous with this type of service. The same goes for Uber Eats. It has become the leading company in the home delivery gourmet industry.

There are similar examples with product names. Xerox - Xeroxing is the word in the US for copying. Or Google, googling for search. Skype for video calls.

All these companies and products have been given legitimacy by their customers and have won their support. Customers make decisions about goods and services before and after their purchase. Their decisions beforehand are based on their expectations raised by marketing, sales, and promotions. What influences their evaluations of the good and service afterward is the quality of the product or service itself.

Functionality[46] of the product/service is an important component of the quality, but only having high spec is not enough. We need a story. Let's take Tokyo Disney Resort as an example. It is widely known that the staff working in the parks are called "cast." This deliberate staging shapes the story and, as a result, leads to confidence in the quality.

Quality is a determining factor in whether a customer will return. The story needs to be continuous from before to after the purchase. More to the point, the story in this case would ideally be guided by the Cause.

---

46 Functionality is the quality of being useful, practical, and right for the purpose for which something was made.

## Create a package plan that scales up tenfold

A shortcut to increasing management performance tenfold is to devise a "tenfold scale-up concept." What you should focus on here is *value*. For example, if you offer a concept that feels ten times more valuable at twice the price, that will surely be a hit.

The *scale*, in this case, means size, quality, coverage, etc. It depends on the industry. Also, let's not forget the customer perspective here. Aiming for 10 times management performance is inherently in the company's interest. But if you think about what you can do to further increase the *value* your customers receive; you can sublimate it to their interest.

I hear that the millennial generation tends to question, "Why would you sell it for twice the price?" They tend to feel, "If we do, we are putting a lot of burden on our customers. Isn't it better for the customer if we cram the product to full for the same price?"

Needless to say, the important thing here is to first present 10 times the value. It makes sense because it sells for twice the price. It's up to the customer to decide whether to buy or not. It's perfectly fine to raise prices on top of providing an overwhelmingly high value. The tendency for young businesspeople to "stay small" is a bit worrisome.

## Leverage with public relations

I already talked about legitimacy. When your surroundings and society recognize that you are legitimate, the world will begin to revolve around you. Again, legitimacy here is about being given the status of "You are the one who should be doing this." There is a saying, "hard act to follow," and that's exactly what it is. However, no one knows if he/she is irreplaceable or not.

If you can have legitimacy in your industry or community, your opportunities will expand quickly. Growing companies are usually given legitimacy. These situations do not arise by chance. They are creating such a situation by themselves. Because they set goals that are derived from their Cause, the strategic ideas and plans that come out of them, as well as the concrete activities, are all rooted in the Cause. Since the Cause is the source of legitimacy, it is through this series of processes that legitimacy is built.

Public relations have a big role to play in strengthening legitimacy. The better you communicate your company's Cause and goals to the world, the stronger your legitimacy will be. What I would like to utilize here is *the power to implant* and *power to nurture*, which constitute *the power to involve and move people*. By communicating your *Gold Vision*, "This is what our company will be like," you are more likely to gain support from your stakeholders.

## Develop leaders who develop leaders

One of the key elements for achieving *one-to-100* is *leader development*. A leader here is not just any leader. It's "a leader who develops leaders."

A company that is doing well in development has these characteristics. Development has become the culture of the company. Development entails a fundamental contradiction. When you develop a person, the possibility of being "overtaken" eventually comes up. You don't want to be let down in the organization by being superseded by the younger generation. So, there are a lot of businesspeople who think that they cannot be proactive in their development.

To prevent this from happening, you need a corporate culture where the bosses will be respected when the person who was developed by them made a big leap forward. The qualities required of a leader can be summed up in *the levels of authenticity*. I already mentioned *the levels of authenticity*. It is an element consisting of *the levels of futurism*, *levels of abstraction*, *a degree of distance from the status quo*, and *the strength/altitude of Cause*.

Those who can raise people are good at "going down" the stairs of the levels of abstraction. They can always think from a field perspective. Of course, they can freely "go up" again right away. In my regular coaching, I advise, like, "Step up a notch and think about it from the perspective of the CEO (executive)." However, this is the epitome of "Easier said than done." Everyone needs a certain amount of practice.

One needs to ascend and descend the stairs of *the levels of abstraction* with agility. Cultivating such a person is what it means to develop "Leaders who develop leaders."

# What is Needed for CEOs and CEO Coaches

## CEO's roles and readiness

Companies vary in size, but for example, can you have the spirit of "*supporting* 10,000 people by yourself?" This must be the load that only those who have experienced it would know. The reason why I use the word *supporting* is because the definition of leadership has somewhat changed in recent years. You could argue that it has always been so, but these days, mainstream thinking is viewing the organization as an "inverted pyramid" that requires *supportive leadership*. The CEO's arms need to be strong enough to support the load. Unless you are trained regularly, you cannot support the inverted pyramid at the critical moment when it needs to count. It is necessary to integrate all kinds of forces, including your spirit, physical strength, and courage. Even if the organization has a pyramid shape, the role of a leader in ordinary times is to support.

The leader of a company must make the supporting state his/her comfort zone. Then you can enjoy the heavy pressure. And in this comfort zone, lies your readiness to accept the spirit of "The buck stops here." In other words, what the president of a large company needs to do is to hold "the comfort zone worthy for the president of a large company."

When corporate misconduct occurs, it is customary that the president and other executives apologize for it at press conferences. Some criticize this as only a show. While I can understand such criticism, I think otherwise, it's really hard to be the head of the organization. I am not sure if I could go there and apologize like these people.

I can protest for them that they are sincerely apologizing. In their mind, some thoughts may pop up, "Why during my term?" or "What bad luck!" Nevertheless, I believe their feeling of apology is real. Because I know that the president of a large company is prepared to take office assuming such a thing could occur.

## What is needed for a coach is authenticity

The coach who supports such a president must have *authenticity*.[47] The coach needs to operate from his/her high *levels of futurism*, *levels of abstraction*, *a degree of distance from the status quo*, and *the strength/altitude of Cause*. This approach will help the client president maintain a high-level perspective, which can be challenging for one individual to sustain.

The CEOs of large corporations are humans, too. Their field of vision may get narrower, and they may feel depressed or upset. The coaches must support the president, who is in such a state, to return to the former high comfort zone and move forward again. Coaches need to possess high efficacy.

For this reason, the coaches' own goals must be high. Since they do everything in the hope of the success of their clients. It is not for those who want to be in the forefront thinking "I want to stand out." and "I want to earn more money." Coaches are in a completely different profession from the fourth batter of a baseball team or rock stars.

Coaches also must accept what the president carries on his/her shoulders—the lives of the tens of thousands of

---

47  In today's world, CEOs started to become the celebrity. It is used for marketing and influencing share prices. Steve Jobs probably was more famous than Apple. Elon Musk is more famous than Tesla. Maybe shareholders know that when they bring such a leader on board as a CEO of a tech company, their share prices will increase 100x, regardless of what he/she does as CEO. Most of the politics is the same. The leaders often play a symbolic role for public acceptance, but the strategy and execution is done by bureaucrats.

Under the fast-changing business and economic environment, the burden that CEOs need to shoulder is becoming larger and larger. I personally believe we are shifting from a powerful charismatic leader who has magic powers to a leader who shows clear vision of the company and at the same time can form a strong team who believes in the future of the organization. Obviously this is task which a single person finds it to be difficult to hold. – Editor employees as well as the satisfaction of millions of customers. Here again, their high goals and high efficacy are essential.

While the president's responsibilities have gradually increased as he/she was promoted to the current position, coaches must be able to take on that load immediately upon receiving the coaching request. This point is often over-looked, but it is important to note

Coaches need to maintain a high level of abstraction to support the president's responsibilities. Coaches also need substantial strength to carry out their jobs. Coach-client rela-tionships usually last a lifetime. That is because coaches deeply get into the client's brain. Ultimately, from my experience, coaching will be done just by the clients' thinking of the coach in their mind. As a coach, the things I say are very simple: "Let's set your goals, and let's increase your efficacy." And "Let's do it together with the people around you." What I do boils down to these two points. Ideally speaking, they don't need to meet me, all they need to do is to go over their notes or read this book. Just remembering me and feeling my presence, the necessary coaching at the moment will be com-pleted. Thus, I say the relationship is lifelong. Of course, if there is a request for face-to-face consultation or talking over coffee, I have no reason to refuse it.

## Your just cause for the world grows
## your business bigger

When the company and the management have a strong and lofty cause, they can wear their authenticity on their sleeve.

I have explained this point in detail in the book. When you can display authenticity, you can gain strong supporters. Then, your cause is transformed into a "just cause." To put it another way, your cause is revealed by launching a "just cause" into the world. Causes tend to be like the roots of a rhizome that sends out extensions in many different places. It is significant to be aware of your cause clearly and to be able to transform it into a "just cause." If you can establish a "just cause," your business will naturally grow.

## The president's spirit shapes the company's happiness

It is all about goals. As the president's goals intermingle with those of management and employees, the company's goals develop. It is important to note that the defining factor of the goals comes from the participating members. An element of the company goal already exists in the brain of each member who gathers, and the goal of the company is established by finding and combining these elements. If the members change, so does the goal of the company. The goal is not something to be forcefully determined by saying, "Let's make this a goal," but rather it is something naturally decided by the members.

It is determined by where heart-to-heart interactions take place among all the members of the organization and where strong vibrations are generated. When the hearts of the president, executives, and employees resonate deeply with one another, the organization's power will be dramatically increased.

## Sending cheers to the presidents

Whether they took office through internal promotion or the succession of a business, many presidents are most passionate on their first day. As they continue, they will be divided into two groups: those who get on the road and maintain it, and those who sigh saying to themselves, "Well, this must be it," as the flame of passion diminishes.

As a promoter of the *one-to-100* concept, I sincerely hope the number of presidents who belong to the former group increases. I want to increase the number of presidents who keep their flame of passion higher and higher and run their businesses happily every day. Even those who feel that their passion at the time of their inauguration is disappearing, it is possible to rekindle it and fully reclaim it. The V-shaped recovery will not be a mere dream and it is possible, don't worry, just practice what is described in this book one by one.

This book is intentionally made as simple as possible, but implementing the contents is not so easy. After all, this book is about *one-to-100*. You would agree that it is a challenging road to go. The other point I would like to emphasize is the aspect of *management by all* in the *one-to-100* concept. There is a limit to what the president can do alone. It might be manageable if the company is currently small, but it will soon become difficult. Let's have as many employees as possible understand the *one-to-100* concept and have them join the circle of management by all. Keep it in mind, though, that the scope of understanding will vary depending on the employee's career, age, job category, and job responsibilities. There may be areas that are too difficult to understand. Still, they will get something, if not all. As they learn it well, they will be able to grasp something more, be influenced, and move forward.

If you use the theories and techniques introduced in this book, you can certainly create a bright and desirable future. It is great that you are in the position to guide employees and staff as the CEO, president, or leader. The path may be challenging, but the time will come when you feel "I am glad we have done it," or "I am happy to have lived through it." So, let's move on, trusting ourselves and our fellow employees.

# ACKNOWLEDGMENT

I want to thank Nihat Karaoglu and T. V. Suresh for their excellent editing and also for the assistance of Dr. Bob Quinn and Christophe Makni for reviewing the book, and also Rie Jindo and Noriko Hosoyamada for translating the book from Japanese to English.

# ABOUT THE AUTHOR

Kazuyoshi Hisano is the president of Conoway Inc., a company specializes in coaching CEOs, organizations, and individuals who want to grow without limits.

He has taught his Gold Vision method to more than 10,000 people and is the founder of the Gold Vision University, established to teach the method. He also teaches coaching programs at Temple University, Japan.

He is the author of *CEO Coaching: How to Grow Without Limits!*, *Gold Vision: See Your Future, Believe in Yourself, Involve and Move People*, and *Feedforward Thinking: Create the Future You Want*, which are published in English by PCS Press.

# INDEX

## E

Examples of organizations where Feedforward has become the norm, 108

Execution, xv, 6, 136

## F

Feedforward meeting, 115, 116

Five elements which determine the level of authenticity, 130

Four stages of management's awareness level, 35

Free yourself from the three constants; "time," "other people," and "money", 69

## G

Get the principle of homeostasis on your side, 93

Goal setting → Taking actions is the basic, 60

Gold Vision Method, 6, 19, 136

Good visualization and bad visualization, 61

## H

Have a high goal (ability to see the future), 73

Hiroshi Aramata, 121

How to create an "environment where you can fail", 143

How to deal with the negative feelings, 75

How to get out of the current state of mind, 48

How to improve your power to believe in yourself, 73

How to turn a one million company into a 100 million company (theory and practice), 181

Human brain, 54, 60, 136

Humans talk to themselves 50,000 times a day (Self-talk), 68

## I

Identifying the essence of a leader, 28

If you don't shift your comfort zone, your organization won't grow, 185

If you grow up too fast, you will miss your step, 191

Important things for not leaving the organization behind, 171

Interviews using future-oriented thinking, 111

Intuition, xxv, xxvi, xxviii, 22, 33, 61, 94, 100, 105, 153, 177, 178, 181

It takes time because you think it will, 190

## K

Keep your efficacy high, 132, 133, 191

Kenichi Ohmae, 20

Konosuke Matsushita, 8, 9, 35

## S



## T



## W

## Y